# The Christian Ministry Series

When I was a publisher I had the privilege of publishing the
I Believe Series and the Jesus Library, working with Michael Green
who was the series editor. It is now a still greater privilege to be
writing this foreword as the series editor for the new Christian
Ministry Series, designed to equip individual Christians and the
local church for effective ministry into the new millennium. The
Christian Ministry Series will explore a wide range of vital issues
for individual Christians and for the Church. The series is committed to excellence, with each book produced by a prominent
leader in their field. Every author will be asked to provide a bedrock
of stimulating biblical reflection, combined with a practical approach
designed to ensure that the particular dimension of Christian
ministry they are exploring has every opportunity to take off both
for individuals and within the local church.

While some will come to the series as a result of a book that
deals with their specialist ministries, we believe that many will
decide that the growing series is a resource that they cannot afford
to be without. The Christian Ministry Series will help readers to
develop and improve their present ministry but will also enable
many to branch out into areas they have never explored before. We
believe that many individual leaders and many local churches will
recognise the value of collecting the entire series, whether to add
to an existing range of resources or to begin such an investment in
resources for effective ministry. In a world of constant and rapid
change, both in society and in the Church, the Christian Ministry
Series will take us back to the unchanging foundations of Scripture
and enable us to move forward with confidence and effectiveness.
My prayer is that these books will release *maximum ministry* in

many churches, not only in Britain but around the world.

During the past quarter century teamwork and team ministry have returned to centre stage. As we have looked again at Jesus and the disciples, Paul and his apostolic teams and Moses with his leaders of tens and hundreds and thousands, we have come to realise that there really is no place in the New Testament for the one-man band. In many settings, however, it has proven easier to give assent to the importance of teams in principle than in practice. Church leaders whose training and professional experience have been in splendid isolation sometimes struggle with the principles of teamwork. Others have discovered in practice the twin dangers of team members who domineer over others through force of personality and the naive assumption that any group of Christians who are thrown together are compatible as an effective team. There is therefore a very considerable need for Christian leaders and writers who can make sense not merely of the concepts but also the delivery of teamwork in the local church.

Justin Dennison has brought to this field a rare combination of expertise. This book demonstrates that he is prodigiously well read in the arena of leadership and teamwork, indeed his doctoral studies were in this field. But Justin is no ivory tower theoretician, for he has also served in teams at several leading churches in Britain and Canada, notably Goldhill, Millmead, Altrincham and Bramalea Baptist Churches. This is a book that recognises the pinnacles and pain of teamwork and will help every reader make the most of the teams in which they play a part. I apply two tests to anything I read about teamwork and leadership, and Justin's book has passed them both with flying colours. He helps the reader reflect more clearly about personal experiences of teamwork, good and bad, so that lessons are learnt for the future. What's more, alongside this clear-sighted analysis he provides practical insights, so that the reader is almost bound to say: 'Now that's an approach I would like to explore in our team!' Justin is to be congratulated upon a book that will prove enriching to many teams in many different kinds of church.

Rob Warner
Queens' Road Church
Wimbledon
February 1996

# Team Ministry

## A Blueprint for Christian Leadership

Justin Dennison

# Hodder & Stoughton
## LONDON   SYDNEY   AUCKLAND

First published in Great Britain 1997

10 9 8 7 6 5 4 3 2 1

British Library Cataloguing in Publication Data
A record for this book is available from the British Library

ISBN 0 340 62484 X

Typeset by Avon Dataset Ltd, Bidford-on-Avon, Warks

Printed and bound in Great Britain by
Cox & Wyman Ltd, Reading, Berks

Hodder and Stoughton
A division of Hodder Headline PLC
338 Euston Road
London NW1 3BH

To those with whom I have had
the privilege of being
part of a team:

Jim, Michael, Len, Peter, Alan, Graham,
Bob, Fred, Steve, John, Pam,
Roger, Judy, Frank, David, Mildred,
Bill, Eileen, Dave, Dean, Ben, Terry, Brian, Gene

To you belong the struggles,
to you belong the spoils!

With special thanks to Sue,
a leader among leaders,
the best teammate
of them all!

# Contents

# Tables and Figures

## Tables

## Figures

# Foreword

'There are three requirements for a good programme within the church. The first is leadership, the second is leadership, and the third is leadership. A lack of leadership may be part of the reason that in a typical year, an average of at least eight Protestant congregations disappear every day . . . Churches need more leaders, not more members.' So wrote Lloyd Perry in 1977 in his book *Getting the Church on Target*. Admittedly he is writing out of his background in the American church, but I would want to change his 'may be part of the reason' to 'is part of the reason'. In fact I believe it to be a major and almost unrivalled reason. Of course preaching is important, worship is important, biblical theology is important, pastoral care is important, evangelism and social action are important. But these remain unfocused, in danger of abuse, and almost certainly incurring energy and money without fruit, unless godly, biblical leadership is there to give direction and destination.

This is a book about leadership by a leader deeply involved in leading, for leaders. It has a wide sweep as it views leadership in general, drawing on scholarly and practical insights from a multitude of backgrounds. This is no superficial, emotive, or subjective work. One is aware of thorough research having been carried out into historical and contemporary thinking on leadership. This gives security in the treatment of the issues addressed. The bibliography is impressive!

Justin Dennison brings to his writing the clinical mind of a scientist who taught science. Recognised early on by his own profession as a leader, he came, in mature years, to a living relationship with God through Jesus Christ. It is out of the reality and warmth of that background that he writes. You will find the contents of the book liberally interspersed with personal experience and illustration as well as scriptural insight. He asks five questions which are mandatory to be answered by every leader – whatever the nature of his leadership:

- Where are you leading your people?
- Do you know where you are going?
- Do your people know where you are going?
- Who has decided the destination?
- Who has decided the route?

As the title of the book indicates Justin writes about the functioning of team leadership. The potential, the richness, and the biblical foundations and examples of the team principle are ably laid down. Practical guidelines are identified and explored. The tensions and conflicts that seem to be inherent in such a concept are confronted with integrity and realism. Here is the voice of someone who knows the pressure, the pain, the confusion of it all. Team ministry would be embraced by most these days as an honourable and profitable way to proceed, yet few would claim a high rate of 'success'. Many would feel bewilderment in the event that things have not worked out as a team yet all the while being convinced that it should have done so.

I was raised in the climate and trained in the concept of the 'one-man ministry'. As I read Justin's book – and it certainly is compelling reading – I found myself wishing that someone had put it into my hands on that Guy Fawkes night forty years ago when I was ordained to the Christian ministry. My journey has brought me to the same destination, but the route I have taken need not have taken so long to discover, nor need I have spent so many fruitless hours in trial and error.

Justin Dennison looks back through the pages of his book and concludes: 'This book has endeavoured to show how a team can keep the momentum moving, and yet still keep the exchanges smooth between the runners.' Because I know the man who wrote it; because it is earthed in local church reality; and because it has a firm biblical foundation, I believe it will achieve just that.

Jim Graham

# Preface

## V is for leadership

The eagle is often depicted as the epitome of leadership. Managerial slogans adorn a dramatic picture of the steely-eyed eagle, peering over the mountains into the sunset beyond. His far-away look and outstretched wings epitomise the mystique of leadership. Majestic in appearance; unruffled by the challenge; alone and aloof; he flies high above the obstacles of the ground; with unflinching determination he journeys towards his destiny.

Yet for all its compelling power, the eagle on reflection is a most inappropriate candidate for a picture of true leadership. Eagles are lone birds, they do not flock, families and mates rarely fly together. They tend to live a solitary existence and therefore lead no one but themselves. Leaders are called to be with others, to influence the behaviour of others, to have followers. Leaders are at the head of a herd, a pack, a team, a group, a flock.

In the context of team ministry it seems to me to be far more appropriate to think of a leader not as a solitary bird but as a bird at the head of a flock. The lead-goose in the 'V' formation of a gaggle of geese migrating to a better climate. As a team, with its leader, honking on their way, their aerodynamic design cuts a powerful swath through the skies. Their mutual co-operation is an admirable demonstration of a team working together. They are a group guided by the inspiration of the leader; each one flying close to the next and making their invaluable contribution.

This book on team ministry is not a manual on how to train eagles to fly together. That approach to teams needs to be put to

xiv

flight! ' "V" is for leadership.' This book is about how a group of simple geese flying in formation, whooping in delight, can cover thousands of miles and live in warmer climates.

This is written for those who have struggled on their own against the headwind; for those who long to fly with others, but don't know how; for those who have flown with the flock but have found the beating of others' wings have buffeted them along the way; for those who hoped to fly high yet found themselves grounded. This is written for those who know there is more to know about themselves, about their teammates and about their God. Ephesians 3:14–21.

# I

# Team players

As a pastor it has been my privilege over the years to counsel many people. On occasions I have spent perhaps an hour or so with a single person who has been struggling with being alone and desperately wanting to be married. They long for all the support, companionship and encouragement a marriage relationship could provide. Ironically, sometimes that very counselling session has been followed by a couple who are struggling with staying together and want their relationship to end. Instead of bringing out the best in each other, as every marriage ideally should, they have sadly discovered that they have been bringing out the worst in each other, as any marriage can surely do. Marriage, in and of itself, is never the panacea for a person's problems and frustrations. Alternatively, being single, to someone trapped in a marriage, can seem to be a very attractive proposition.

So it is with the Christian ministry. There are those toiling away on their own who long for a worker/leader to come alongside them and share the burden and responsibility of ministry. They dream of the Shangri-la of team ministry. Team ministry will surely, they surmise, be the answer to all their problems and frustrations. On the other hand there are those involved in team ministry who have become so disillusioned, discouraged and disheartened by the experience that they want a divorce for it has become a living hell.

I have also noticed over the years that in some marriages two people can be living together under the same roof, eat at the same meal table, sleep in the same bed, share the same bathroom, watch the same television set, drive the same car and yet in actuality be living miles apart. They are a married couple living together like two single people. I have discovered that the same is true with some team ministries. The name is used, the theory is propagated, yet the reality is two or more people working in the same church or organisation yet not really working together as a true team. Their team ministry is more 'talk than walk'.

Marriage should be a joy. As someone who has been married for twenty years, I know it certainly is! What a privilege to have someone alongside you as a supporter, encourager, partner and confidant. It is a blessing that goes beyond words. I thank God for the gift of my wife Sue – where would I be without her?! I also thank God for the blessing of having others alongside me in the ministry – where would I be without them?!

But as in a marriage so in ministry, I counsel people to think carefully before committing themselves and joining their lives closely with another. Whatever the type of leadership team – be it pastoral, missionary, organisational or lay – it is delightful if relationships are healthy, but destructive if they are not. So make sure you go in with your eyes wide open!

My own observation – as someone who has pastored for twenty years, and been a member of four different church pastoral teams – is that the process of joining a team and becoming part of that team can feel like a marriage. The trauma of leaving a team, or experiencing a team member leave, can feel at best, like a bereavement; at worst, like a divorce. Nevertheless, I still remain undeniably optimistic about teams and hopelessly committed to team ministry! For, beyond all else, it is my firm conviction that it is clearly not biblical to think of ministering alone.

## Biblical basis for team ministry

The Bible provides today's Church with a blueprint for effective ministry. Through living examples, a picture of how ministry is to be accomplished is painted and presented to the Church. Admittedly, the culture and context in which the events took place are separated from today's Church both in time and space. Nevertheless, the underlying principles of how to proclaim the gospel effectively and so to build the Church remain unchanged.

The constant challenge for the Church in each generation is to take the unchanging principles and precedents of Scripture and contextualise them into the ministry environment of the day.

The Church in every age is commissioned with the awesome responsibility to present Christ as a living witness to its own generation worldwide. However, 'God's work must be done in God's way to receive God's blessing.' The Scriptures provide the framework upon which today's Church must be founded and formed if it is to be effective, fruitful and faithful in its calling. One such solid foundation stone is the bedrock of team ministry.

### The first team

On the opening page of Scripture the first team is brought into being. Adam and Eve reflect the *Imago Dei*. 'So God created man in his own image . . . male and female he created them' (Gen. 1:27). It could be argued that the Trinity is the first team. It certainly is the perfect team, in fact the only perfect team in existence! God reflected the profound truth of Team Trinity by creating the team of Adam and Eve. God placed Adam in the Garden of Eden and gave him the responsibility of cultivating and caring for it. With such a daunting task set before Adam, God declared, 'It is not good for the man to be alone. I will make a helper suitable for him' (Gen. 2:18). Faced with the challenge of ministry, the first human team is formed – a couple who will complement and encourage one another in the task placed before them.

The phrase 'suitable helper' or 'helpmeet' is difficult to translate succinctly. It conveys the notion of someone who comes alongside another in companionship and support, complementing the partnership in a unique and beneficial way. It draws out the best in the other and so enables them to fulfil their full potential because of the closeness of the relationship. Although clearly a beautiful picture of the marriage bond, it is also an insight into all close relationships. The creation account clearly emphasises the principle of team ministry. It was admittedly founded in the marriage relationship, but Adam and Eve were more than simply the procreators of the human race. They were co-workers, co-labourers, and team members in the Garden of God.

The apostle Paul, in underlining the importance of team ministry, draws a similar picture when he writes,

> The Lord has assigned to each his task. I planted the seed, Apollos watered it, but God made it grow. So neither he who plants nor he who waters is anything, but only God, who makes things grow. The man who plants and the man who waters have one purpose, and each will be rewarded according to his own labour. For we are God's fellow-workers; you are God's field. (1 Cor. 3:5–9)

## The great ones

It is very evident, as the pages of Scripture unfurl, that whenever God placed a significant responsibility upon the shoulders of a person, he inevitably gathered a team around that person. Throughout the Old Testament this principle is demonstrated on a number of significant occasions in the life and history of the people of God.

When God called Moses to the task of liberating his people from the bondage of the Egyptians he was called while alone, but he was immediately placed in a team with Aaron (Exod. 4:14). Each was assigned a specific task; Moses was given the responsibility of listening to God, while Aaron was given the task of speaking for God. Throughout the Exodus account the names of Moses and Aaron are consistently linked together. Indeed as events unfold the team is increased. Miriam is added as a prophetess and praise leader (Exod. 15:20–1). The two eldest sons of Aaron, Nadab and Abihu, as well as the seventy elders of Israel are also mentioned (Exod. 24:1). In the same passage Joshua, described as Moses' aide in verse thirteen, is also included. Joshua's appearance on the scene marks the point where he begins to play an increasingly significant role alongside Moses and before the people.

Throughout the Exodus story there is a team of at least two people, sometimes up to five, working together. Over the journey, the team changed in numbers and composition under the constant leadership of Moses. This flexible approach to team ministry appears to characterise significant and lasting biblical teams, as we will notice later with the apostle Paul.

## Home and away

The exilic return was another momentous event in the history of Israel. The account stresses the part that team ministry played in the success of the venture. During the Exile we read of the lives of Daniel, Hananiah, Mishael and Azariah (Belteshazzar, Shadrach, Meshach and Abednego), the latter three men always mentioned synomously together (Dan. 1–3). The Scriptures indicate that without each other they could not have achieved what they did for God and for his people. Esther and Mordecai could be another example from the same period illustrating another aspect of team ministry.

The success of the return was due to three great consecutive leaders: Zerubbabel, Ezra and Nehemiah. Yet each one did not operate on his own. Ezra lists a leadership team of eleven people, which includes Zerubbabel, Joshua, and Nehemiah (Ezra 2:2). Zerubbabel, the governor, was aided directly by Joshua, the two being linked together as a team on a number of occasions, for example, 'These are the two who are anointed to serve the Lord of all the earth' (Zech. 4:14). Alongside them the twin prophets of Haggai and Zechariah made a formidable team (Ezra 5:1). Ezra clearly worked as a team leader alongside eleven others (Ezra 8:16).

Nehemiah was also clearly a team player. The plural of the personal pronoun – 'we', 'us' and 'our' – is used throughout his account. He organised the task by appointing teams of people along specific sections of the wall. He too mentions Zerubbabel's full team (Neh. 7:11). He also worked closely with Hanani after the walls were rebuilt, and mentions the prominent part played by Ezra in the renewal of God's people. There are many powerful and practical insights concerning leadership in general, and teamwork in particular, that can be gleaned from this part of Israel's history. The leader of any team, church or organisation would find their time well spent and profitably rewarded through the study of this part of God's Word.

### The perfect team player

Throughout the ministry of Jesus we discover many of the principles that produce a great team player. Jesus was not an independent operator but was accountable to and under the authority of his Father, 'I tell you the truth, the Son can do nothing by himself; he can do only what he sees his Father doing, because whatever the Father does the Son also does' (John 5:19).

He realised that he needed the help of others to fulfil his earthly ministry. He would then be able to hand the baton on to them to ensure that his ministry continued after he returned to heaven. So Jesus chose his divergent team of twelve disciples, a veritable mixed bag of talent and gift-mix. He chose prayerfully, carefully and wisely, 'That they might be with him and that he might send them out to preach and to have authority' (Mark 3:13–19). In turn he instilled in them, from the very beginning, the necessity for team work by sending them out to minister in teams, two by two (Mark 6:7; Luke 10:1).

Jesus also had a smaller inner team, a cabinet core of leaders: Peter, James and John (Mark 9:2; 13:33). He was especially close to them, and passed on to them the primary corporate responsibility of leading the Church after his departure. The early church leaders were therefore discipled by Jesus in many ways, not the least of which being the principles and practise of team ministry. It is generally acknowledged that Jesus exemplified what many today would regard as the necessary qualities and skills for successful team leadership.

## The team player par excellence

The book of Acts and the apostolic epistles provide the clearest picture for today's Church of how ministry is to be done. The mode of team ministry found in the history of their ancestors in the Old Testament, demonstrated by their Lord Jesus during his ministry, clearly shaped and characterised the life of the Early Church. In the light of all the examples given above, this should not be a surprise. What should cause a raised eyebrow is that the supreme example of a team player found in the infant Church should be one who on the surface seemed to be such a complete, competent and competitive individualist – none other than the incomparable apostle Paul! Yet the team approach to ministry is clearly demonstrated in the book of Acts. It is rare indeed to find the early apostles engaged in ministry alone. In fact, the team approach to ministry is exemplified more by Paul than by any other apostle.

Throughout Paul's ministry there is a series of distinct teams which reflect a flexible and fluctuating approach to team ministry. The formation of these teams indicates a clear intention to minister alongside others. On those rare occasions in which he ministered alone it appears to have been dictated more by circumstances than by choice. Some of his teams were together for many years, others were quite short-lived. There appears to be a basic team around Paul with the addition of short-term members as the need arose. Each additional team member obviously changed the dynamics within a team and so in the process created in effect a new team.

A study of the book of Acts and the Pauline epistles shows that Paul can be identified as a member of at least twelve different teams. There is a great variety of formation and duration. The members were together for varying lengths of time, and some members branched off en route to form their own teams and so multiply the ministry. Other team members remained in places where a church had been founded to establish and pastor it, often working alongside others. So some of the teams could be considered as part-time lay leadership teams, whereas others are clearly full-time pastoral or missionary teams.

### Team 1. Barnabas, Saul, and John Mark (Acts 13:4–13)

This team was sent out by the church at Antioch with Barnabas as the team leader. In addition to fulfilling their mission, Barnabas also used the opportunity to nurture and mentor Saul. The public ministry was always shared between them, but as the journey continued Paul became the main speaker. This was the classic intern/associate pastor or missionary model in action. Paul also encountered his first team failure when John Mark left them to return to Jerusalem (Acts 13:13).

### Team 2. Paul, Barnabas, Judas, and Silas (Acts 15:22–43)

Even though Barnabas is on the team, Paul is now the leader. In the process of discipleship, the reins of responsibility have been handed over to him. The commitment to team ministry shown here by Barnabas is impressive. Barnabas, who was the mature Christian and initially the mentor of Paul, was subsequently prepared to become his follower. It takes a mature person with a commitment to people and team ministry to step aside as Barnabas did. He certainly lived up to his nickname, 'Son of Encouragement'! Two new members, Judas and Silas, were specifically chosen for the task that lay before Paul. The public ministry continued to be shared by all the team members.

### Team 3. Paul and Silas (Acts 15:36–41)

Paul had obviously felt let down when Mark left them on their previous journey (Acts 13:13). So when Barnabas suggested that he join them again, Paul and Barnabas 'had such a sharp disagreement that they parted company' (Acts 15:39). Here we find the honesty of Scripture recording this team-split between two of the Early Church's major leaders. The disagreement birthed another team, so although it did divide the ministry, it also multiplied it. There is disagreement among commentators as to who was in the right and who was in the wrong. The important point to focus on, however, is not that they separated, but why they separated. For disagreements within a team do not necessarily always indicate right and wrong positions. There was an element of truth in each of the opposing views held by Paul and Barnabas. They found themselves on opposite ends of 'the work/the worker' or 'the mission/the man' spectrum. Paul was clearly more task-orientated, whereas Barnabas was more people-orientated. Their disagreement and parting were due more to a clash of team principle rather than to a personality clash.

### Team 4. Paul, Silas, Luke, and Timothy (Acts 16:1–17:34)

Luke now joined Paul and Silas, and the 'we' passages commence (Acts 16:10). Paul also selected Timothy to join with them. Paul clearly noticed great potential in this young man and spent the next fifteen years discipling and mentoring him as an integral part of many teams. During this period the team showed tremendous flexibility. Paul ministered together with all the others; sometimes with only Silas; occasionally on his own, as he did in Athens; Silas and Timothy ministered together apart from Paul.

*Team 5. Paul, Silas, Timothy, Priscilla, and Aquila (Acts 18:2–23)*

This team was formed in Corinth following the founding of the church in that city. Two local lay leaders, Priscilla and Aquila, initially worked alongside Paul until Silas and Timothy arrived and rejoined the team. This couple became the mainstay of the church after Paul and his team moved on. They in turn established Apollos, the pastor-teacher in the ministry at Corinth. Here we see a fine picture of the discipleship of nationals. The baton of leadership is passed from missionary to lay leaders to local pastor.

*Team 6. Paul, Timothy, Erastus, Gaius, and Aristarchus (Acts 19:21–41)*

Paul now added three new members to the team, Erastus, Gaius and Aristarchus. Not a great deal is known about these men, but each of them served long and faithfully with Paul on several teams for many years.

*Team 7. Paul, Timothy, Tertius, Gaius, Erastus, and Quartus (Romans 16:21–24)*

The letter to the Romans was written towards the end of Paul's third missionary journey from the city of Ephesus. The way the names are listed does cause some speculation about the exact composition of the team. In all likelihood, the people mentioned reflect those who Paul had on his itinerant team, as well as those who joined him in the leadership team of the local church. Some argue that there are two teams and not one found here. It seems more likely, however, that the nature of Paul's ministry at that time required a flexible approach to the team membership.

*Team 8. Paul, Timothy, Luke, Sopater, Secundas, Gaius, Aristarchus,*
*Tychicus, and Trophimus (Acts 20:4)*

This was one of the largest and most diverse of all of Paul's teams.
It had an international flavour as it was drawn from a variety of
ethnic, cultural and geographical backgrounds. Paul enlisted team
members as he travelled. He observed them at work in the local
church he had established, and then he used them to establish other
churches. He was therefore able to prove and test a person's gifting
for ministry in general, and suitability for team ministry with him
in particular. Paul exemplified that the biblical way and true testing
of a person's call to missionary work is to observe the effectiveness
of their ministry in their own culture prior to sending them into
another culture. A proven track record of ministry in a team setting
is one of the most vital evidences of a call to Christian ministry,
whether as a missionary, pastor or leadership team member.

*Team 9. Paul, Luke, and Aristarchus (Acts 27:2)*

On the long and arduous journey to Rome, Paul needed the support
and encouragement of his other team members. His ambition to
reach Rome was being realised but not in the way that he had
envisaged. He would arrive free in Christ, but a prisoner of Rome.
It was a difficult time for Paul. So having pastored and encouraged
others, it was now time for others to encourage and minister to
him.

*Team 10. Paul, Tychicus, Onesimus, Aristarchus, Mark, Justus,*
*Epaphras, Luke, and Demas (Colossians 4:7–14, Ephesians 6:21)*

In his prison epistles to the Colossian and Ephesian churches, Paul
had clearly not set aside his commitment to team ministry. He was
no longer at liberty to travel where he liked, but he directed others
to continue to spread the gospel freely. Through his writings and
personal ministry he was therefore ensuring that after his departure
the effectiveness of his ministry would continue to impact the
Gentile world for Christ. He exemplified what it means to be a

good athlete of Jesus Christ by passing on the baton of faith safely to others (2 Tim. 2:2, 5).

### Team 11. Paul, Demas, Crescens, Titus, Luke, Erastus, and Trophimus (2 Timothy 4:9–12, 19–21)

The theory that Paul enjoyed a brief release from his prison in Rome to travel into Asia Minor has, according to Donald Guthrie, 'been embraced by almost all scholars'.[1] Paul's team seems to have included the above people. In his second letter to Timothy he explains how his team has been dispersed. Titus, who had been with Paul for several years, has become a key church leader. He is mentioned in the Galatian and Corinthian epistles, and he was Paul's messenger to the Corinthian church. Evidence is scarce but he had undoubtedly been a companion of Paul for many years, so this in all probability was not his first team experience. Paul had groomed Titus, along with many others, into the place where they could be entrusted to pioneer their own missions and team ministries.

### Team 12. Paul and Luke (2 Timothy 4:11)

Assuming this letter is written shortly before his death, then Paul still had his team in place. His trusted friend, companion and historian Luke was still with him to encourage, support and minister to his personal needs. The cycle had gone full circle. The minister is now in need of ministry, the pastor in need of pastoring. The genius of team ministry continued to flourish although the responsibilities and roles of its members may have changed over the years.

### Principles from Paul's team ministry

There are several key lessons that emerge from the study of Paul the team player/leader and the teams in which he played such a vital part.

1. They were commissioned by and accountable to the local church.
2. They were guided by the Spirit and corporate guidance.
3. Their primary focus was on vision, the task at hand.
4. They displayed a wide diversity of gifts.
5. They were intentional and deliberate in purpose.
6. They were changing and dynamic in membership.
7. They showed flexibility in incorporating new members.
8. They were multicultural in nature.
9. They were intimate in their relationships.
10. They modelled authority: brother, yet also father and mother.
11. They used on-the-job training through mentoring and doing ministry.
12. They were resilient through adversity.
13. They reinstated former failures, giving them new opportunities.
14. They practised disengagement when the task was completed.
15. Many members stayed together often for several years.
16. They formed deep and lasting relationships.

## The biblical model

Paul is often portrayed as an individualist yet, as we have seen, there are twelve different teams of which he was a member. There are another twenty-two teams referred to in the New Testament. It is, therefore, no surprise that when churches go back to the Scriptures for a fresh study on Christian leadership and church structures, they invariably implement a model which reflects team leadership.

Team ministry is a biblical concept which underpins the pages of Scripture. In Paul's letter to the Ephesians, the great treatise on the Church, it is perhaps most clearly spelled out. Paul writes in Ephesians 4:10–12 describing examples of the leadership gifts that Christ has given to the Church: people such as apostles, prophets, evangelists, pastors and teachers. They were given, not to do all the work, but to equip others to be workers so that the body of Christ may be built up. Team leadership and team membership are beautifully combined. Westing rightly points out, 'It is logical to conclude, therefore, that Christ expected it would take a team of people to build the church.'[2]

# 2

# Team spirit

Teams are everywhere: in sports, in music, in families, in factories, in businesses, in companies, in clubs, in churches. But what does it really mean? The word 'team' conveys a variety of meanings to different people. So what is meant by the word in general, and by extension, what should a church pastoral team or Christian leadership team be in particular?

## Defining team ministry

A team has been variously defined as:

T.E.A.M.: Together Everyone Achieves More.

Teamwork: Coming together is a beginning. Keeping together is progress. Working together is success.

Teamwork is the ability to work together toward a common vision, the ability to direct individual accomplishment toward organizational objectives. It is the fuel that allows common people to attain uncommon results. Simply stated, it is less me and more *we*.[1]

The *Chambers Dictionary* suggests the following definitions:

Team: A set of persons who have joined forces with others,

working in combination to make a co-operative effort.

Team spirit: A spirit of self-suppression in co-operation.

Team work: Work done by organised division of labour through co-operation and pulling together, with regard to success of the whole rather than personal exploits.[2]

During an away-day our pastoral team at Bramalea Baptist Church discussed the process of team building and together we created the following definition which was then approved by our deacons' board:

A team is a group of diversely gifted people, who complement one another, and who feel called by God to be committed to work together toward an agreed vision, which is otherwise unobtainable. This involves the willingness of team members first, to subordinate individual accomplishments and personal preferences in order to achieve the common goal; second, to be accountable to and to submit to the appointed leadership of the church.

There are several key elements which define a team:

1. Commitment to an agreed common vision and purpose.
2. Good and honest communication between members.
3. Individuals with complementing talents/gifts/contri-butions.
4. Subordination of the individual for the common goal/good.
5. Combined effort, which multiplies group effectiveness and produces an increased individual creativity.
6. An interdependent and submissive spirit by all members.
7. An appointed and recognised leader.

I believe that a team, by definition, must have a recognised leader. The role of a leader may vary considerably from one team to another, but it is essential that their position and authority is accepted by all the other team members. The team will thus remain focused on its vision and stay a cohesive and effective unit. A team without a leader is like a ship without a rudder; it is at the mercy of the elements and it will eventually be blown off course.

## Team advantage

There are several advantages for a person who is part of a team. Ben Sawatsky makes the observation: 'There are two basic reasons for joining a team. First, the team approach has the support of biblical precedent, and second, the team approach results in healthier, more well-rounded ministry products.'[3]

### 1. Complementing gifts

A constellation of abilities, skills and experience are inevitably found. This gives a person the freedom and ability to focus on their areas of strength. This reduces the pressure to excel in all areas and so avoids the frustration of being placed into ministries which do not fit.

### 2. Ministry strengths

A person can play to their strengths and focus on their ministry gifting. Few people, even on a team, will ever have the luxury of spending 100 per cent of their time and effort exclusively in one area. A team affords the person the opportunity to devote most of their time and to stay focused on their main ministry. Don Cousins, the former associate pastor of Willow Creek Community Church in South Barrington, Illinois, says that there is an expression used frequently in the corridors of that church. People speak of the '70/ 30 rule'. He maintains that a person should be devoting 70 per cent of their time into the area in which God has called and gifted them.[4] There are others who say that more realistically this should be 60/40. Whatever the figure, team ministry enables a person to minister primarily in their area of strength.

### 3. Gift development

People grow when ministering alongside others as there is opportunity for relevant and informed feedback. Honest evaluation can be done by those who work closely alongside one another. Ministry doors can open to other opportunities as encouragement is given by those gifted in other areas.

### 4. Support system

Emotional support may be needed, as we all experience both highs and lows, success and failure, crisis and discouragement. Spiritual support can be an effective deterrent against temptation through mutual accountability. Physical support combats loneliness and isolation. Some people can function alone more easily than others, but nevertheless, everyone needs fellowship and friendship.

### 5. Intensifies vision

Team members can keep reminding each other of their vision and keep each other focused on the bigger picture.

### 6. Greater productivity

The sheer multiplication of gifts, skills, experience and manpower will generate greater confidence to take on a major assignment. This is one of the most compelling by-products and raison d'être of team ministry. A lone cart-horse can pull two tons; two cart-horses teamed together can pull five times that amount. Coming together in a team causes an increase in the capacity and productivity which goes beyond the combined sum of the lone individuals' efforts. Biologists call this phenomenon 'synergism'. They use it to describe the action of two or more organisms achieving an effect far greater than the sum of their efforts measured independently. A team of three or four people can achieve far more and make a far greater impact than the same number of individuals working alone. Solomon knew the wisdom of this when he said, 'Though one may be overpowered, two can defend themselves. A cord of three strands is not easily broken' (Eccles. 4:9–12).

## Ideal team size

What is the ideal team size? A team can be too large, or it can be too small. It is said that, 'Two's company, three's a crowd', but in the context of a team it is fair to say that, 'Two's company, three's a team, and more than fifteen is a crowd!' Research in small group dynamics suggests that eight is the optimum figure. This enables good communication, deep relationships, a pool of creativity, with variety of gifts and personalities. Moses, however, divided up the people of Israel by tens. Jesus had his twelve disciples, and the Early Church followed his example in Acts 1. Yet they appointed seven 'deacons' in Acts 6. Jesus also sent his disciples out two by two. As we have noticed, each of Paul's teams had a different number, depending on the circumstances.

The optimum number appears to be anywhere from eight to twelve. There does not seem to be a biblical precept on the matter. The precise number will be determined by the practicalities (usually financial) and the purpose of the team. I have worked in pastoral teams of two to eight people; on church leadership teams of twelve to twenty; on mission boards of six to eight. I did find some of them too small and intense, others too large and impersonal! Lay leadership teams, meeting once or twice a month, can be much larger than full-time pastors/people who are working closely together every day. A church lay leadership team of about twelve would seem to be the maximum effective number. A pastoral team larger than about eight would need an altered management approach to maintain a true team spirit. A team of two can also be very effective in pastoral ministry, but I think three is better, and Ecclesiastes 4:12 supports my view!

David Cormack lists some of the disadvantages of different sized teams:

## Larger teams

1. Difficulty in selecting people who will fit.
2. The likelihood of frequent membership change.
3. Finding roles and tasks for each member which match their skills.
4. Communication between so many allows for misinterpretation.
5. Arranging meeting times acceptable to all.
6. Developing one-to-one relationship.
7. Developing members' skills.
8. Allowing sufficient time for members to contribute.
9. The dangers of sub-group formation and conflict.

## Smaller teams

1. Insufficient resources.
2. Limited skills.
3. Lack of creativity.
4. Poor problem solving.[5]

## Pitfalls in team ministry

We have to be realistic as well as idealistic. Pitfalls await the unwary. Here are some of the more prevalent disadvantages and potential problems in being part of a team:

1. Exclusive relationships so that the team becomes a clique.
2. A tendency to focus inwardly on its own needs and goals.
3. A self-sufficient, independent and isolationist attitude.
4. An elitist mentality which sets the team above others.
5. The suppression of individual creativity and expression.
6. Consumption of time which deflects from time involved in hands-on ministry.
7. Closeness and intensity of teamwork can cause strained relationships.

There are also, however, destructive elements that undermine team health such as:

1. Unrealistic expectations: meeting of personal needs; resolution of personal insecurities/unresolved problems; being closest friends.
2. Hidden personal agendas: personal ambition; insecurities; reservations about team strategy or philosophy of ministry; lack of loyalty to team leader.
3. Competitive spirit: personal recognition; personal kingdom building; seeking personal reputation, rank or reward.

Team ministry is indeed like marriage – it can be very challenging at times, and we need to be honest about that. Yet, in my experience, both marriage and team ministry are rewarding, fulfilling and positive experiences. I am so grateful to God that I do not have to live alone nor minister alone.

### Staying glued together

What keeps a team together? What is the glue that keeps different people united together, bonded to the task? Harold Westing maintains that for a team to work well together there must be some common elements which can be used to evaluate the team's progress and gauge the group's growth. He suggests the following as measurements of a team:

1. Shared sense of belonging
   Do members feel they belong to the group, are respected, and made welcome?
2. Shared achievement
   Can members see their individual achievement contributing to the 'mosaic' of the team's work, so to the total teamwork?
3. Shared understanding
   Do they understand the deeper background of each other, to see beyond the superficial and so interpret reactions

as coming from the other's culture, education and, experience?

4. Shared accountability
Has the team designed a way to let people get their 'goofs' and 'glows' on the carpet and share them in honest prayer? Who is accountable to whom, and do they both know and accept that?

5. Shared ideas, insights and feelings
Can team members express to each other their thinking, their learning from experiences, deepest feelings, joy, disappointments, despair, frustration, exultation?

6. Shared theological reflection and prayer
Can the team take time periodically for serious study and discussion? Does the team see prayer as a help in making decisions, to 'work through' a problem, so being open to the Spirit's teaching them?[6]

## Assessing strengths and weaknesses

It is one thing to define what a team is. It is quite another to get a team working together. How is one to ascertain whether the team is working well, whether it is healthy? No one is perfect so, by extension, no team can possibly be perfect. What constitutes healthy imperfection, and what constitutes unhealthy symptoms? What are the indicators of the natural struggle to grow together, and what indicates stunted growth or the terminal sickness of a team?

Although no test can ever be truly objective, Ervin Henkelmann and Stephen Carter, in *How to Develop a Team Ministry and Make It Work* maintain you can achieve a 'Team Ministry Quotient' (TMQ) by evaluating ten key characteristics or elements of 'teamness'. Each element can be evaluated and given a score out of ten, added up and then the team can be given a TMQ rating out of one hundred.[7] The ten characteristics are:

*1. Recognition of roles:*

roles and responsibilities are known and agreed; job descriptions;

clear expectations; an acceptance of authority and leadership; commitment to team concept; respect for diversity.

## 2. *Channels of communication:*

openness with each other; time to talk and listen; clear lines of communication; printed information; agreed decision-making procedures; team involved with and informed of all necessary changes; established times for meetings.

## 3. *Strength of relationships:*

climate of care; considerate and courteous; differences respected and enjoyed; loyalty; accommodating; no pressure to conform; time together socially; a sense of belonging; sense of togetherness; growing together; harmonious personal relationships; healthy balance of relationship and task.

## 4. *Handling of differences:*

operate out of a servanthood style; respect and appreciation; healthy interaction; disagreements and conflict acknowledged, worked through and resolved; weaknesses and strengths are recognised; ministry never manipulative; differences kept within the team.

## 5. *Measure of security:*

high expectations; hard work; long hours; quality results; excellence in ministry; growing professionally; openness to change and new styles of ministry; good morale; appropriate public recognition and credit given where appropriate; salaries proportionate to responsibilities.

## 6. *Common vision:*

job bigger than the team; committed to overall task and pulling together; willingness to help where needed most; clearly defined purpose and agreed goals; enthusiastic; flexibility; optimistic; unreserved commitment; enjoy working together.

## 7. *Mutual support:*

respect individuality, but not individualistic; concern for success of other's programmes; encouragement, support and affirmation of others' ministries; helping each other over rough spots and towards personal growth; mutual trust, support, respect and appreciation.

## 8. *Climate of creativity:*

using all member's resources; ministering in areas of strength; growing in spiritual giftedness; increased team effectiveness and creativity; excellence; acceptance of other's spiritual gifts; ensure competencies are not unused; accessible but not drawn away from own responsibilities; total member ministry approach.

## 9. *Transparency and teachability:*

no room for suspicion; rely on each other; comfortably confide; work at being genuine; mutual accountability; acceptance of own strengths and weaknesses; open and receptive to feedback; regular review and evalution.

## 10. *Communal worship:*

a spiritual foundation to ministry; team involvement at Sunday services; pray together when meet together; meet for devotions regularly; worship together is meaningful and helpful; desire to grow together personally and spiritually.

* * *

I have used the TMQ to evaluate each of the pastoral teams of which I have been a member. It can be used as an inventory of team health, perhaps at an annual team retreat. It is also a valuable tool for any prospective new team member to ascertain their commitment to team ministry, and to convey to them the current health of the team.

Table 1. Team Ministry Quotient[8]

| | | |
|---|---|---|
| 1. | Recognition of roles | /10 |
| 2. | Channels of communication | /10 |
| 3. | Strength of relationships | /10 |
| 4. | Handling of conflict | /10 |
| 5. | Measure of security | /10 |
| 6. | Common vision | /10 |
| 7. | Mutual support | /10 |
| 8. | Climate of creativity | /10 |
| 9. | Transparency and teachability | /10 |
| 10. | Communal worship | /10 |
| | TMQ = | /100 |

The TMQ as such can never be an objective assessment, but only a relative indication of how a team is doing. It is a single snapshot at a specific time which reveals how the team members view the team. Different members of a team may vary considerably one from the other in how high or low they score themselves.

Each team member should initially complete the test on their own. The whole team should then meet and through a discussion collectively complete the test. A comparison should then be made between the total team score and each individual team member's score. This in itself is a very valuable exercise and should quickly highlight any particular problem areas that may be present. Several TMQs for the same team over of period a time would then provide a more accurate assessment of the 'teamness' of the team. The team should do the test each year. Then the results may be compared with those of the previous year and indeed over several years. In this way any weaknesses, frustrations or problem areas should be easily identifiable and brought to light. The team then has the responsibility and opportunity to grow and deal with the situation and so increase their effectiveness as a team.


## S.T.E.A.M.

It is usually obvious when an orchestra is not in harmony, or a football team is not playing well together. It is sometimes harder to spot immediately when a ministry team is not well synchronised, but eventually it will surely surface. It takes patience and practice to play well together and to bring out the best in each other. There are lessons to learn and skills to use, but there are no short cuts to the task of working at becoming a team. 'Practice does make perfect' and so it is with being part of a team. The effort and commitment involved are more than compensated for by the experience of a person achieving something far greater than they could possibly have accomplished by themselves.

We have noticed that one succinct definition of team is: 'T.E.A.M.: Together Everyone Achieves More.' As we are people involved in a variety of expressions of Christian team ministries, let me now add the letter 'S' for the word 'Spiritual'. This now adds the all-important vital ingredient of the spiritual dimension and now spells the powerful word: 'S.T.E.A.M.: Spiritually Together Everyone Achieves More.'

Steam is a mighty force which, when correctly harnessed and channelled, has the potential to accomplish a great deal. It has the ability to enable us to achieve far more than we could ever do left to our own energies and devices. Steam also dissipates quickly, so in order to stay effective it needs to be continually replaced. So it is with the Spirit in our lives. Teamwork is hard work. We need all the help we can get! God offers us that help so he can achieve his plans and purposes through us. With God's ongoing help a team which is constantly connected to him and to each other not only has the potential, but also has the real possibility to be a powerful and effective unit for extending the kingdom of God. A team filled with, and dependent upon, the Spirit is a sharp tool in the hands of our God.

# 3

# Team leadership

Everyone I talk to seems to bemoan the fact that there is a dearth of leadership right across our society today, whether that be in the government or in the church. How often have you heard it said in your church: 'There is so much more we could be doing, if only we had the right leaders! The ministry is being hampered because we can't find the necessary leader!' Sounds familiar? Almost every church I know seems to be in short supply of this invaluable yet basic commodity of church life. Yet leaders do exist, if only we knew what to look for and where to look. It has been said that 'Leadership is like the abominable snowman – whose footprints are everywhere, but who can never quite be tracked down!'

## What is leadership?

Defining leadership is not an easy task. Field Marshal Lord Montgomery of Alamein, the great military leader, said: 'Leadership is the capacity to rally men and women to a common purpose, and the character which inspires confidence.'[1] Eugene Habecker, in the Christian context, defines leaders as: 'Persons who believe they can and must make a difference in their organizations, their families, and their communities, and who do so by following biblical principles . . . the ends or objectives aspired to in leadership must also be biblical.'[2] Calvin Miller speaks of leaders as those who have the three ingredients in God's recipe of: '1. Inward Substance.

2. Outward Daring. 3. Magnetic Motivation.'[3]

A young man at Bible college came to talk to me because he felt that he possessed neither the gift nor the call to church leadership. 'How can I tell if I am a leader?' he asked me. A middle-aged man in our church came to see me because he was being asked to take on a leadership postion but felt he was not a leader. He too asked, 'How can I tell if I am a leader?' In both cases I put it to them like this:

Leaders are those who sit in the pew and observe what is going on and talk to themselves. They hear themselves saying, 'Things could be done differently, things should be done differently. There is untapped potential here. I would involve more people. I could change things and do it differently. I would be prepared to make it different, to make it better, to make it happen.' What they say to themselves is not in an arrogant or criticising way, for it comes from a pure heart and from deep within. They have eyes to see 'what is' and vision to see 'what could be'.

The college student told me he had never thought like that. I suggested to him that perhaps, as he suspected, God was not calling him to a position of church leadership and that God had something else in store for him. The middle-aged man, who had never viewed himself as leader, said, 'I think like that all the time!' I encouraged him to accept the responsibility being offered to him, and to use his unique gifts and personality to influence those in our church.

## Leadership defined

What makes a person a leader? What is it about a person that inspires others to follow them? How could you identify someone in your church as being a potential leader? The spiritual gift of leadership involves the following four vital elements:

### 1. A leader influences people

There is something about a leader which inspires respect and confidence. For some inexplicable reason people are prepared to listen. It often has nothing to do with appearance, voice, stature, learning, title, position or even age, although these can give a person an additional initial edge. Unless this leadership quality is there, eventually the person's views will be politely ignored.

## 2. A leader shapes people's behaviour

This is probably the most telling quality. A Christian leader is always trying to change people. This involves behavioural changes of all kinds, such as church structures, worship patterns, attitudes, lifestyle, etc. Supremely a leader seeks to change others into being Christ-like. That change may involve several steps along the way. A leader shapes and moulds people into godliness. A Christian leader like the apostle Paul should be able to say, 'Imitate me as I imitate Christ' (1 Cor. 4:16; 1 Thess. 1:6).

## 3. A leader inspires towards vision

Leaders have the ability to harness the energy of individuals towards accomplishing a common goal. They possess the ability to inspire confidence in individuals to believe in themselves, to believe in their church, to believe in their leaders and supremely to believe in their God. They have the ability to see a vision through with a dogged determination which ensures their vision becomes flesh.

## 4. A leader enables others to fulfil their potential

The teaching of Paul in Ephesians 4: 7–16 should be a key Scripture for all leaders. Leaders are not to do all the work of ministry, but to equip others to be involved in the work of ministry (verse 12). Leaders are not appointed to do all the work. In the words of John Wesley: 'Don't do the work of ten men, but put ten men to work!' Leaders have the ability to inspire others to gather around and share the load and so all grow in Christ (verse 16). A leader enables their followers to become all they can be in Christ.

These four qualities define the nature of true and full leadership.

They provide a rounded definition which covers the basic essentials of measuring effective leadership. Some people may have one or two present, but if you are looking for front-line leaders then all four are needed.

## Leader or manager?

There is an important distinction between management and leadership. These are often thought of as being the same. However, they are not.

Paul Hersey and Kenneth Blanchard, in their classic work *Management of Organizational Behavior*, point out that management and leadership are often thought of as one and the same. They maintain that there is an important distinction between the two: 'Management is a special kind of leadership . . . whereas in essence, leadership is a broader concept than management.'[4]

Warren Bennis and Burt Nanus, in *Leaders: The Strategies for Taking Charge*, state the difference succinctly by saying: 'Managers are people who do things right and leaders are people who do the right thing.'[5]

### Table 2. Leader or Manager?

| Managers | Leaders |
|---|---|
| people who do things right | people who do the right thing |
| they are efficient | they are influencers |
| carry out the vision | cause the birth of the vision |
| they are implementers | they are inspirers |
| follow through decisions | make the decisions |
| see the goals through | determine the goals |

Leadership is a broader concept than management. An effective leader needs also to be a good manager. A great manager, however, is not necessarily a good leader. For management is working with and through individuals or a group to accomplish predetermined goals. Leadership has to do with the setting of those goals and the direction of the group. From Paul's teaching in the pastoral epistles, and so into church government, I would categorise elders as the church leaders, and deacons as the church managers. Both are involved in a spiritual ministry, but their gifting and responsiblities differ.

These distinctions are crucial, for the effective church leader must be able both to manage and to lead. Many pastors, missionaries, vicars, elders, deacons, etc. seem to function more as managers rather than as leaders. They are maintainers (managers), they are not movers and shakers (leaders). I have also observed that, conversely, some of those with leadership ability are weak in implementing their vision into the life of their church. Leadership involves management: not necessarily being personally and practically done by the leader, but the leader must ensure that it is being done. Failure to do this means that a leader's vision will remain just that – a dream. It's good to dream dreams about what God can and wants to do among his people. It's great to have visions for his work. But both need to be worked at and worked out into the life of the church.

## Negative leadership

Leadership occurs whenever anyone attempts to influence the behaviour of others and as a result causes others to change. We need to recognise that this can be both positive and negative. King David is a great example of positive leadership, whereas his grandson Rehoboam is a good example of negative leadership. During the Second World War, Britain was inspired by the positive leadership of Winston Churchill, whereas Germany was led astray by Hitler, who is probably the best-known example of negative leadership.

Similarly the exercise of leadership in church life can be neither positive nor from the appointed church leadership. We use expressions such as: ringleaders; being led astray; being led up the garden path; being led like a lamb. These expressions demonstrate that people are being profoundly influenced by someone to behave in a certain way, which is neither helpful nor positive. How true in many of our churches! Ringleaders in our churches need to be identified, challenged and influenced (that is led) into becoming followers of the true church leadership.

On the other hand, there are those who view themselves as self-appointed leaders. They will maintain that they have the gift of leadership which they feel called and compelled to exercise. But 'You are not a leader unless someone is following you!' Self-proclaimed leaders often function out of an insecure personality which covets public recognition to bolster their personal self-image.

Both ringleaders and pseudo-leaders – if left alone – will stir up a hornets' nest of discontent, sending people flurrying in different directions, causing pain and frustration for all concerned. Exercise your leadership and deal with them before they wreak havoc and do any more damage!

### Nature or nurture?

There is much discussion today as to whether leaders are born or whether they are made. There are those who believe that leadership is a matter of birth. A person is a leader by nature, they are born and not made. This is the 'Great Man' theory of leadership. Inheritance and destiny make them a leader. Those who had the right breeding could lead, all others must be led. Either you were born with it or you weren't. No amount of learning or yearning could change your ability or your fate.

Another notion is that great events make leaders of otherwise ordinary people. This 'Big Bang' theory suggests that the situation and the followers combined to produce a leader. A crisis propels a person to assume the mantle of leadership which otherwise they would not have taken up. Leadership may be called forth by a crisis, but it can never be produced by a crisis. Did Nazi Germany produce Winston Churchill? Certainly not, but it released him into a new sphere of leadership and authority. No crisis can create leadership. It can only awaken the locked-in latent potential that was always there.

It is also very popular today to say that leadership is something we all can have. It can be learnt. 'Leadership seems to be the marshalling of skills possessed by a majority but used by a minority. But it's something that can be learned by anyone, taught to everyone, denied to no one.'[6]

### Leaders – 'L' and 'l'

Warren Bennis and Burt Nanus painstakingly researched ninety top leaders across a wide spectrum of responsibilities: in business, industry, government, education, and sport. They searched for underlying patterns of personality, physique, background, style, etc. They found no obvious patterns for their success. They concluded that there was a marrow of leadership behaviour which they all embodied, which can be learned, developed, and improved upon. They readily admit, however, that only a few will lead nations, but more will lead companies and many more will lead departments or small groups. They also concede that, as with other complex skills, some people do start out with more fully formed abilities than others and that there are different levels of leadership, so a person may have the ability to be the leader of one kind of team, but may not be equipped to lead another.

Eugene Habecker cites the Harvard professor John Knotter who distinguishes between capital 'L' leaders (of which there are not very many) and small 'l' leaders (of which there are many). He makes the point that: 'It would help greatly (in terms of leadership development) if we would get more people to think about leadership in the small "l" sense. Unfortunately, many people think about leadership in only the capital "L" sense. Yet both capital "L" and small "l" leaders influence others toward a given end, goal or purpose.'[7]

I agree that there is no leadership stereotype, nor a stereotypical leadership personality. Yet I still believe that not all are gifted and called to exercise leadership. We need to acknowledge the fact that some may make great managers ('l' leaders), but be poor leaders ('L' Leaders). Many may function as effective managers, but only a few inspire and motivate others to greater heights by their leadership.

### *Charisma* and *chrisma*

I believe that leaders are born and made. I also believe that leadership can be learned but it can never be taught. A leader has to hone and refine the gift that God has already given. If a person does not have the gift there, however great or small the talent is, then you can neither give it to them nor can you teach it to them. Some people are born with a musical gift, but they still have spend hours a day to learn how to play the violin. No amount of teaching would ever transform me into a Yehudi Menuhin or a Nigel Kennedy! So it is with leadership. I have worked with and trained many people over the years, and a willing heart does not equal a gifted soul. What God endows by nature, however, a leader must

Table 3. Leaders – Born and Made

Nature and nurture
Gift and grace
*Charisma* and *chrisma*
Leaders – born and made
Leadership – always learnt but never taught

nurture. Jesus's teaching on the parable of the talents in Matthew 25: 14–30 illustrates this well. God's gifts also need God's grace in order for a leader's potential to fully realised. Jesus may gift a person (*charisma*), but Jesus also needs to continue to work in and through that gift (*chrisma*). Leaders need to learn to be leaders. Leadership is not simply a matter of genes or heredity, nor can it be manufactured. It is not the product of some neat and nifty methodology. That is why 'Leadership is always learnt, but it can never be taught.'

## Recognising the gifted leader

We should, however, beware of stereotyping the gift of leadership. There is no one right leadership style or personality. Secular research and the Scriptures show that leaders come in all shapes and sizes, in all types of personality, with varying styles, from all walks of life, and in both genders. Admittedly, only a few will lead national organisations, but some will lead denominations, more will lead churches, and many more will lead small groups and church ministries. Just as there are different styles of leadership, there are also varying levels of leadership. There are those called to lead ten, others a hundred, others a thousand, and still others tens of thousands. A person may have the ability to be the leader of one kind of group, but may not be equipped to lead another.

Many may make great and effective managers, but be ineffective leaders, for the exercise of the true gift of leadership will inspire and motivate others to greater heights. I believe that true leaders are like cream: they will always rise to the top. A natural mover and shaker will not sit still in the stands for long. They will want to be on the field and call the play. So start stirring and shaking others into action! Whatever leadership position you hold in your church, God has called you to influence and shape the behaviour of those you lead. So don't be timid. Stir up the gift God has given you (2 Tim. 1:6–7).

Leadership is for those God calls, who then with outstretched hands are ready to receive and ready to give; who are willing to serve and who are willing to learn; who are willing to step forward from the safety of the ranks and make a difference. The God-given talent of leadership will never reach its full potential without a teachable spirit and the willingness to hone and refine that gift.

## *The* leader or *a* leader?

By definition a team is incomplete without a leader. At the end of the day, someone needs to be responsible for ensuring that the team makes the right decisions, and that they are implemented. Both Scripture and experience show that every team needs a captain – an appointed and recognised leader. A good leader, however, leads not by being 'over' his teammates, but by being 'among' them. He is not their superior and they his subordinates – they are all co-workers in Christ. The team members are fellow-labourers; he may lead them but he does not lord it over them.

Not so long ago I heard of a senior pastor who had to work through a very difficult conflict situation with another pastor on his team. His commitment to the principle of team ministry meant that he was known as the senior pastor; those who worked with him were known as associate pastors, not assistant pastors. He was keen to reduce the differential that had existed in the church between senior and associate/assistant pastors in the past. Although he was officially the senior pastor he was often referred to as simply the pastor of the church, which he welcomed. His associates were often referred to as pastors of the church. Looking back he now recognises that in his idealism, born out of a genuine desire for team ministry and a wish to erode an overemphasised pastoral hierarchy, he had planted the seed of false ambition in the mind of one of his associates. It was a painful lesson for him.

He noticed after a year together, that the associate (and his wife) would refer to himself as *the*, not *a*, pastor of the church. It seemed trivial, but after several weeks the senior pastor challenged him on this. He was told that it was simple semantics, he should not be so insecure and suspicious! Foolishly, he was reluctant to force the issue and confront the problem that was obviously there. It all came to head within a year or so during a discussion with the deacons in which the associate maintained that he and the senior pastor were equal partners in the team. He had to be reminded who was the senior pastor and who was the associate pastor. The key issue was that he had great reluctance in accepting his role as an associate and the senior pastor as the team leader. He did not regard the senior pastor as *the* pastor and himself as *a* pastor; to him they were equal associates, both simply pastors. Neither the deacons nor the senior pastor agreed with his view. Of course the real issue was that the associate had a struggle in submitting to leadership.

An unfortunate experience? Yes, indeed! An extreme experience? No question! A difficult team situation? Without a doubt! An unusual conflict? Unfortunately not, for I have sadly discovered that in Christian ministry similar stories abound.

## Watch your language!

The language a team leader uses will often reveal, beyond all the rhetoric, what they really believe inside. Some team leaders will talk of the team as being co-workers, but they constantly refer to team members as 'those who work under me' rather than 'those who work alongside me'. Whatever may be said, the actuality is that they view themselves as the boss, surrounded by subordinates. For this reason I have always referred to the members of my pastoral teams as 'associates' and not as 'assistants'. The team members do not work 'under' me, but 'alongside' me. I am not their 'boss' but I am their leader. The technical term for this approach to team ministry leadership is *'primus inter pares'*, which is Latin for 'first among equals'. It seeks to model both the biblical principles of authority and servanthood by the team leader, and accountability and submission by the team members. The leader is, of course, also a team member and must therefore also demonstrate mutual accountability and mutual submission.

I believe that team leadership is a way of working – not a way of showing power or preference. The leader takes on a burden and does not assume privileges. Christian leaders can so often mimic the world rather than the biblical model of servant leadership by lording it over others, rather than working with them; by drawing attention to themselves and grabbing the credit for what is a team achievement. Every leadership team – be it a pastoral team, eldership, deacon board, missions board, etc. – is like a string quartet, needing one good lead which the others can clearly follow. That lead, however, must appreciate that the three other parts are needed to produce the desired musical harmony. The leader may be the spokesman, but he must not not always stand out as the only player and so receive all the accolades and credit. In this way true harmony and unity are maintained in a team.

### It's a funny old game!

A few years ago I was the chaplain to Manchester United Football Club. I am also a fan of American gridiron football, I support the Miami Dolphins. A comparison between the two types of football illustrates well the point I wish to make about team leadership. In American football the coach is the one who usually calls the plays. He normally communicates these to his quarterback, the captain on the field of play, who is the star player. In the team huddle there is no discussion between the players. The quarterback tells them what play has been decided. It is their responsibility to run their routes and so execute the play. In other words, the leadership style of American football is one-way, directive and hierarchical. Perhaps this is why so many American pastors and leaders tend to follow this sports model of leadership!

In European football, the captain's role is different. He is chosen by virtue of his experience and expertise at motivating others and not by his position on the pitch or field. He is not usually the star of the team. He is given the final responsibility for making decisions on the field: who should take free kicks, penalties and so on. If he is wise, he will consult with his other leading players and gain from their wisdom and experience. His aim is to get the best from all the players on the field. He must mould and motivate them into playing, not simply as group of great individuals who happen to be on the pitch at the same time, but as a collective team.

It is not unknown for a premier league team with an array of great stars to be beaten by a third division team of part-timers in an FA Cup replay. One team were playing as a team, the others as a collection of individuals on the same pitch. When a team plays well together the individual team players' talents and individuality need not be suppressed. As they play with and for each other they can be enabled to perform to the best of their ability in their given positions. In this way, individual fulfilment and team success can go forward together hand in hand. The leadership style is two-way, participatory and relational. Perhaps that is why many British church leaders have a more egalitarian approach to team ministry. Interestingly, this style of team leadership is the one that is now being propounded by the present-day mananagement gurus from every continent.

## Different strokes for different folks

Ask the average person in the street to give you an example of leadership, and the chances are that the names of Margaret Thatcher, Winston Churchill, Desert Stormin' Norman Schwartzkopf, John F. Kennedy and so on, will quickly be mentioned. People will probably say that the problem with some of our politicians is that they are definitely not leadership material! Most people have stereotyped what they think a leader should be and should do. When they think of a leader they probably have a particular type of person and a particular approach in mind. Yet all the research concerning leadership shows that there is no one type of leadership personality, nor one type of leadership style. Effective leaders are not all cast from the same mould. There is no one right leadership style or personality. Leaders come in all shapes and sizes, are both introverted or extroverted, come from all age groups, from all walks of life and from both sexes. Effective leaders clearly do certain basic things well, but they are not necessarily all alike.

The style of the leader should not be stereotyped. A leader of one team may vary their approach from that of a leader in another team, depending on the situation. The way that a leader interacts with one team member may be different to the way in which they interact with others in the team. Indeed the dynamic of a leader's relationship may change with the same individual team member over a period of time. Paul Hersey in *The Situational Leader* points out that:

> For every job there is an appropriate tool . . . to build effectively you need a variety of tools and the knowledge of what they are designed to accomplish. The same is true of leadership and management. It is unrealistic to think that a single tool is all that's needed to manage effectively. . . . You need to understand and be able to use different tools when leading and managing people.[8]

Paul reminds us that all the gifts or charisma (including that of leadership) are given to many in a variety of different forms, yet it is the same Spirit who gives and who is at work (1 Cor. 12:4–6). Most management gurus today maintain that there is a spectrum of leadership styles which can be represented by the extremes of leader-centred or group-centred, with a balanced style in the middle.

### 1. Leader-centred style

This is an authoritarian approach which tends to inhibit the growth of those 'under' them. People become dependent on the leader and unable to operate without him. The problem is that this tends to promote the thinking that there is only one brain in the group – the leader's! Creative thinking is suppressed, and eventually the leader runs short of ideas. The leader has also to constantly supervise those 'under' him to ensure they do as they are told! The advantages to this style are that people know who is in charge and the direction they are going and that the job gets done.

## 2. Group-centred style

This approach may cover up the inconsistency and incompetency of a weak leader because it focuses on the interests and relationships of those 'alongside' the leader. Yet it too is fraught with difficulties and frustration. The leader struggles to make decisions and so is difficult to pin down. Those 'alongside' him do not always respect or trust his authority and so tend to fend for themselves. The task is not usually done well which fosters low morale. People, however, feel listened to, they relish the opportunity to get on and do something, and they enjoy being together.

## 3. Balanced style

Between these two extremes there is a balanced approach, which is dynamic and responsive to the needs and abilities of those being led, the task at hand, and the needs and abilities of the leader. This approach involves the use of all brains present so that creative thinking is stimulated. Full discussion of problems and involvement of those being led is encouraged. Consultation, joint decision-making and delegation of responsibilities would be prevalent. This style encourages a climate which is supportive of innovation and change. People feel wanted and so have a strong sense of belonging, which in turn means that the work at hand gets done well and effectively.

### Situational leadership

Paul Hersey and Kenneth Blanchard (of *The One Minute Manager*) have developed a model of leadership which they describe as 'situational leadership'. This has now become accepted by leadership consultants as one of the most helpful models of understanding and applying leadership. Hersey and Blanchard maintain that there is no single way which is best in influencing or leading people. People are different, companies are different, churches are different, teams and team members are different, and so the situation in which a

leader is placed, and their response to it, must also be different. The
effective leader is the one who is able to adapt their leadership style
to meet the demands of the situation. Many leaders make the
elementary mistake of adopting the same style of leadership within
a wide range of contexts and with a variety of people. The
leadership approach that a person adopts, with individuals or
teams, will depend on the aptitude level of the people the leader is
attempting to influence.

Situational leadership is a dynamic model in which the
behaviour of the followers determines the leader's behaviour.
Hersey and Blanchard maintain that there are four basic
approaches to leadership, depending on the dynamics of the
situation. The behaviour of the leader ('leadership style') is
dependent upon the ability and willingness of those in the team
('follower readiness'). The amount of direction the leader gives and
the follower assumes are therefore related. The amount of guidance
('task behavior') in proportion to support ('relationship behavior')
that the leader gives those following, changes as the leadership
approach varies. Situational leadership styles are:

1. *Directing/telling – structure and supervision*
You do through them: guiding and establishing.

2. *Coaching/selling – explain and clarify*
You do together: persuading and motivating.

3. *Supporting/participating – listen and facilitate*
They do, you encourage: collaborating and participating.

4. *Delegating/monitoring – self-directive*
They do, accountable to you: observing and fulfilling.[9]

I have adapted Hersey and Blanchard's diagram, so see Leadership
Resources for an expanded version of their model.

The situational leadership approach has proved to be
appropriate for a variety of settings: business, industry, education,
government, military and even the family. It has helped people
appreciate the changing role in parenting. Parental control has to
alter as children grow older, so that children mature to the point of

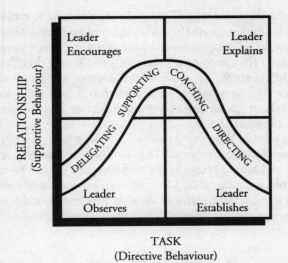

*Figure 1. Situational Leadership Model*[10]

being able to make the right decisions for themselves. Similarly, it is an appropriate model for all forms of Christian leadership. Team leaders need to be those who encourage others in the maturing process, and so releasing others into further ministry and future leadership opportunities. Leaders should 'Let my people go!' and by so doing they will 'Let my people grow!'

Effective team leaders are those who, like the apostle Paul, can say, 'I have . . . been all things to all . . . men that . . . I might win some' (1 Cor. 9:22 J. B. Phillips). Skilful leaders are those who do not view the people they lead or their own leadership approach as all cast in the same mould. They do not cast themselves or others in concrete and stereotype their leadership style but change it to meet the dynamic challenges of the situation. Effective leaders recognise that there are 'different strokes for different folks' and what is more, that there are 'different strokes even for the same folks'! People do change over time. The way in which they can handle responsibility, and indeed the amount they can shoulder, will or may change.

Some team leaders have a tendency to approach everyone and

every situation the same way. They assume they have a leadership style, which is God-given and immutable, and to which others must yield and mould. Having pastored four different congregations I quickly realised that each new group of people and their leaders were very different. What worked well somewhere else was not going to have the same effect in a new church setting. I had to adjust my style of leadership to remain effective and to meet the demands of the situation.

There is no doubt that we all have a leadership style or approach with which we feel most naturally comfortable, or even secure. The truly skilful and secure leader is the one who can break the mould and be flexible and adaptable. He or she can thus move beyond the restrictions of a one-dimensional view of leadership and learn to live and move in the four-dimensional situational approach.

### Be a chameleon for Christ!

The chameleon is a lizard-like creature which changes its skin colour to blend into its background and so remain camouflaged. Now, without pressing this analogy too far, I believe that leaders can learn an invaluable lesson from the chameleon: leaders do need to stand up and stand out, but they also need to be able to blend into their surroundings, to be relevant and sensitive to those around them, in order to be effective. If you are a leader, then there is a sense in which at times you should 'Be a chameleon for Christ!'

### Follow my leader

What conclusions can be drawn in the light of all the above insights concerning leadership in general and the role and character of the team leader in particular?

1. Not all have the gift of leadership. In some it may lie dormant, in others its full potential is yet to be realised. Both nature and nurture need to play their part.

2. There is no one type of leader nor one type of leadership style or personality. The gift or *charisma* of

leadership is given to many in a variety of different forms.

3. There is no right or wrong style of leadership behaviour.
4. Leaders must assess the demands of the situation and adopt the most appropriate style for the given circumstances.
5. An effective leader is one who can operate across the leadership-style continuum and can modify it appropriately for each given situation.
6. The people being led need a consistent and clear style of leadership. Any changes in style or approach need to be carefully explained by the leader.
7. Leadership is also about 'followership'. A leader can only be successful if allowed to lead. Even the best of leaders will be comparatively ineffective unless those being led have a submissive and co-operative spirit and are willing to follow.

# 4

# Team leader

A daunting task faced me when I arrived at my present church almost three years ago. The church had been without a pastor for three and a half years, the people were discouraged, there was so much to do. The first thing, however, that I determined to do was to seek God for a fresh vision for the ministry there, and to pass this vision on to the church members. It has been a slow process, but now there is a different atmosphere about the place. There is an excitement and expectancy that God is moving again among us. Effective leadership has been the key.

## Seven leadership distinctives

I believe that there are seven fundamental distinctives which characterise the effective Christian leader.

### 1st leadership distinctive – be a person of vision

First and foremost a leader must be a visionary.

> All men dream; but not equally.
> Those who dream by night
> in the dusty recesses of their minds,
> awake to find that it was vanity;
> But the dreamers of day are dangerous men,

that they may act their dreams with open eyes
to make it possible.[1]

The change in our church began with a fresh vision from God for
his work. Vision is seeing beyond what has already been
accomplished in the past to what God desires for the future. As a
leader, God's desire needs to become my desire. Leaders do not rest
on the laurels of past achievements, but have a sense of expectancy
that God wants to do even more in and through the lives of his
people (Eph. 3:20–21; Phil. 3:12–15).

Leaders must be men and women who have a burden to seek
and know God's will for their work and a commitment to do it.
Vision is to see beyond the limitations of the present and to see
what is possible with God. Robert Schuller speaks of leaders as
being 'possibility thinkers'[2] who open their minds to God to unfold
his will. God can then perform miracles in people who, unafraid
of failure and public embarrassment, move boldly and bravely
forward attempting big things for God and expecting great things
from God.

### Vision: spiritual insight – to see as God sees
Vision is to see as God sees, it is spiritual insight. Vision is to have
a clear God-given sense of direction and purpose, coupled with a
commitment to complete the journey. Vision is to look beyond the
limitations and frustrations of the present and to see what is
possible with God. Spiritual vision, however, is not having good
ideas manufactured by people, or copied from elsewhere; it is being
inspired by God's Spirit. This is a vital distinction for us to grasp
in our franchise-minded culture. Vision is Spirit-initiated, not
people-motivated. Because it is implanted by God, God also
imparts the faith to believe it can happen, and the power to see it
through.

Vision is to have the certainty that this is what God wants
done. True vision, born of God, grips a person like a vice and
will not let go until the job is done. It has been said that
'Unless you see it, before you see it, you will never see it!' That
statement requires some thought, but it contains a real nugget of
truth!

James Belasco and Ralph Stayer, in their imaginative book on team leadership *The Flight of the Buffalo*, put it well:

> Vision is the beginning point for leading the journey. Vision inspires and touches the heart. Vision is our alarm clock in the morning, our caffeine in the evening . . . Vision becomes the glasses that tightly focus all of our sights and actions on that which we want to be tomorrow, not what we were yesterday or what we are today.[3]

Do you have a vision for the work to which God has called you to give leadership? The crucial questions for you to reflect on are: 'Where am I leading my people?' 'Do I know where I am going?' 'Do my people know where we are going?' 'Who has decided the destination?' 'Who has decided the route?'

Paul Beasley-Murray makes the point that:

> Leaders are those who are imbued with the spirit enshrined in the words of George Bernard Shaw, 'You see things as they are and ask "Why?" But I dream things that never were, and ask, "Why not?" ' . . . Leaders are great optimists, but optimists in the best sense of the word: for suffering neither from false optimism, which ignores or dismisses problems, nor from pessimism, which allows people to be crippled by the problems that are around them, visionary leaders are those who see the problems in the light of God.[4]

For every leader, vision is the vital guiding principle. People follow leaders who have vision, who know God and know what God has planned and purposed for his people. The leader therefore pulls rather than pushes people on. The leader influences and motivates by attracting and energising people to identify with an exciting vision of the future. It has been said that leaders acquire and wear their visions like clothes.[5] What are you wearing? What do your people see? I encourage and challenge you to put on the fresh clothes of vision. Dress yourself with the insights of God, and as you lead, others will follow God who is upon you.

### Be a firelighter, not just a fire-fighter
One of the frustrations of being in leadership is that you can spend

so much of your time being a fire-fighter instead of being a firelighter! Leaders who are fire-fighters are those who are constantly reacting to situations, trying to pour oil on troubled waters, pacify this person or calm down that person. They discover that it is a never-ending task, for as soon as one fire is put out, another one breaks out somewhere else! God's purpose for his leaders is to have men and women who are primarily firelighters – people who light the fire of vision in the hearts and lives of those they lead. God's desire is for leaders to devote the bulk of their time not to dousing the fires of discontent but instead to 'fan into flame' what he wants to do among his people (2 Tim. 1:6).

It is vital for leaders to have clearly in their minds who they represent. In our democratic society, we elect our leaders to represent our views, our postion, our needs; they become our voice in high places. Sadly, in many churches our church leaders are regarded in the same light, as spiritual lobbyists. Leaders are viewed as those who are there to safeguard the different interest groups and segments of the congregation, to ensure every voice is heard and championed in the corridors of power. Leaders, however, should be consumed with what God wants of them rather than overly concerned about what others want them to do. It is not a question of 'What do *they* think?' but 'What does *he* think?'

### Be a God-fearer, not a people-pleaser

When faced with challenges and difficult decisions, leaders should not focus on the question, 'How will people react?' but rather, 'What does God want us to do?' It is the finding and carrying out of God's will that becomes the determining factor, not the fear of strong-willed people within the church. This is not meant to imply that leaders should be insensitive or indifferent to the needs of those they lead. Leaders do need to be in touch with the concerns of those they lead, they do need to be listening to the flock and leading them gently. Above all, leaders need to be listening to and hearing the Shepherd's voice. Leaders need to be God-driven, not driven by the voice of the vocal minority or the unstilled voices of the discontented, or frozen into inactivity by fear of people's reaction. Leaders need, like Paul, to be God-fearers, not people-pleasers (Gal. 1:10, 1 Thess. 2:4). Leaders are those who discern and discover the will and vision of God for his people.

*2nd leadership distinctive – communicate your vision*

Vision in leaders is, in and of itself, insufficient. Leaders must also be able to communicate God's will or vision in a way which convinces and compels their followers to follow their God-given lead. The second key leadership characteristic of leaders is the ability to articulate and communicate God's vision to his people. The fire that has been lit in their hearts and minds by the Spirit of God has to be lit in the hearts and minds of others. The vision has to be articulated until it has caught fire. The team leader, whatever their title, should remain the prime articulator of the vision, but all members of the leadership team should be involved in the dissemination process. Communication can be done through words, graphically through pictures, creatively through banners, encapsulated in catchy phrases or slogans. Whatever it takes for others to catch the vision and not to lose sight of it must be done. People's imaginations need to be captured and fired up if faith is to be released and flourish. People need to be excited by the possibility of what God can do and wants to do among them corporately and through them individually.

Effective communication takes an abstract vision, earths it and makes it live in the hearts and in the minds of people. Effective communication changes the way people view themselves and the way they view the future. It generates a climate of confidence and creates a healthy self-esteem which produces a 'we can do it' mentality. Confidence breeds confidence, so vision needs to be shared with an enthusiasm which excites others with what is possible and enthuses them with the necessary commitment to complete the task.

On the mountain top, the leader receives vision. Down in the valley, the leader's task is communication.

In seeking to lead or influence others through communication, there are three steps through which a leader needs to take people.

1.  Give them a clear understanding of what the situation is now and what you believe it can be in the future.
2.  Show them the discrepancy between the two, which is the arena of challenge and faith.
3.  Explain the process of change, which will close the gap

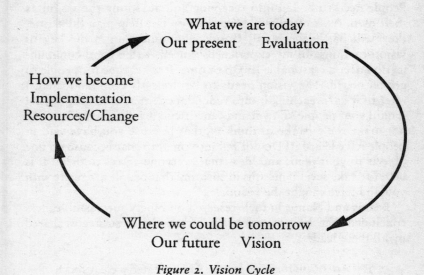

Figure 2. *Vision Cycle*

between the current situation and what you believe God wants you all to achieve together.

These steps need to be communicated in such a way that people can easily understand and accept them. Even if you understand the situation, if you are unable to communicate that effectively, the whole process will not have the impact you would like it to have. Sharing the vision requires patience and persistence. It involves discussion and if necessary, refining, until people reach that place in which the vision becomes not 'theirs', but 'ours'. A vital transfer has to occur. God transfers his vision to leaders, who receive it, grasp it, and run with it. In turn this baton of vision has to be passed on to the people who must also receive it, grasp it and then run on with it. The vision has therefore become owned and not imposed on them from above by the leadership.

Pass on the baton of vision from leadership to ownership.

The process of transferring leadership to ownership is a vital one and must not be rushed until the transfer is safely completed. Many a leader has rushed the hand-over to his people and discovered, to his anguish down the road, that the baton has been dropped. People need to be led into receiving and accepting the vision as their own. As is often said, 'If people do not help plan the battle, they will battle the plan!' Good communication is the key to vision-catching. In my experience, it needs to be good communication over a reasonable length of time. It takes time for people to get on board. The vision needs to be tirelessly communicated. I refer to it as 'preaching it into redundancy'; that is to keep saying it until your people know it and can articulate it for themselves. Do not make the mistake of thinking that because you have said it, people have heard it! Do not fall into the trap that because no one objects to your plans and ideas that everyone agrees to them! It is better to take several months in ensuring that people are really with you and have caught the vision.

Bennis and Nanus in their research on ninety successful leaders concluded that there were four characteristics or strategies shared by all these leaders.

1.  *Attention through vision.* They created a clear focus of compelling intensity which produced a magnetic willingness to follow them.
2.  *Meaning through communication.* They used compelling images that induced enthusiasm and commitment to the vision.
3.  *Trust and innovation through dedication and reliability.* They inspired others which enabled them to implement challenges and change the basic metabolism of the group.
4.  *Contagious attitude.* They had a positive and optimistic approach to others and to the future.[6]

If these observations are true in the secular field, how much more should they characterise the leaders of God's people!

Our church's vision is kept constantly before our people. I never take it for granted that everyone will automatically know it. It is summarised on small cards which we give out every year. It is depicted on a large banner which is displayed in our foyer and often placed on the platform of our church. Our vision symbol is on the front of our visitors' welcome card. It is often put on the front of our church bulletin. Every year, during the month of September, at the restart of the church year, I remind our people of our vision, and underline what we believe we need to emphasise and focus on for the coming year. All the above are reminders, a stake in the ground, to both long-standing members of our congregation and to newcomers, that this is where God is leading and directing us. His vision is our vision, and by his grace we will not lose sight of it. This is especially important when it comes to implementing change in a church or Christian organisation. Vision which is caught paves the way for change.

## 3rd leadership distinctive – be a change agent

James Belasco in his management bestseller *Teaching the Elephant to Dance* bases his book on the interesting fact that trainers shackle young elephants with heavy chains to deeply embedded stakes. In that way the elephant learns to stay in its place. Older elephants never try to leave even though they have the strength to pull up the stake and move. Their conditioning limits their movements so that with only a small metal bracelet around their foot, attached to nothing, the elephant will not move far. Belasco maintains that like powerful elephants, many organisations are bound by earlier conditioned constraints. 'We've always done it this way' is as limiting to progress as the unattached chain around the elephant's foot. Success can tie you to the past. The very factors that produced today's success often create tomorrow's failure. Belasco observes that organisations are like elephants, slow to change, and that too many have metal bracelets around their feet which limit their progress.[7]

## Implementing change with the minimum of pain

What is true for elephants and companies is almost certainly true of most churches and Christian organisations. As we have noticed, by definition a leader is a person who is able to influence the behaviour of others, and as a result cause them to change. Christian leaders are those who have a God-given vision and who lead those around them into that vision. Christian leadership should therefore, above all else, be vision-driven and not maintenance-

minded. Implementing change with the minimum of pain is one of
the constant challenges and frustrations of being in leadership. Yet
God has called leaders to be those who move people on from those
restraints, real and imaginary, which tie them to the past and so
obscure their vision of what God has for them in the future.

## Change agent

The renowned church consultant, Lyle Schaller, says that every
church leader should be a 'change agent'.[8] In other words, leaders
should view themselves as those who encourage others in the
constant process of change. A leader has to be prepared to 'comfort
the disturbed, and disturb the comfortable!' If you are in leadership
this means implementing vision, which will inevitably mean
implementing change. Being a 'change agent' is not always easy or
popular. We are all creatures of habit, and indeed tradition, even if
we're young, so we all struggle to some degree with change. In fact,
in a world which is constantly changing at an ever-increasing pace,
there are those who look to the Church to be an unchangeable rock
in a sea of shifting sand – 'All may change, but nothing changes
here!'

   It is essential for people who are following you that they see
clearly the necessity for any particular change. It is not 'Change for
change's sake', but rather 'Change for vision's sake'! Vision creates
a clear tomorrow. 'Change agents' create a clear today. It is vital
that your people see the present situation as it really is. Stir up the
complacency and disturb their comfortableness by honest and
candid reflection on what is really happening around them. This
will often help people to realise that change is not just inevitable,
but also essential. I refer to this process as 'increasing the climate
of discontent'. Ask awkward questions about why certain
programmes are being done and how they are being done. Get your
people to question the what, the why, the how, the when, the who
about your church life. If you can get people discontented with the
present and envisioned for the future, you have prepared them for
change. By building a sense of urgency you will show the necessity
for change.

   Your people must be led, not pushed or dragged into change.
Change isn't easy, there are often significant obstacles to overcome,
not the least of which is inertia. The people you lead must come to

that place in which they sense and feel the urgency so that 'To change or not to change?' is no longer the question but it is 'How to change?' Given vision, time, patience and the grace of God, people will see for themselves that there are better ways of doing things; there is a better place in which their church, under God, can be. They will move from being comfortable and contented to being more open to change. Vision is the focus for change, but urgency will provide the energy to achieve it.

Vision creates a clear tomorrow. Change agents create a clear today.

Belasco uses the powerful imagery of an elephant being inside a circus tent to encourage change. If the tent catches on fire, and the elephant sees the flames with its own eyes, and smells the smoke with its own nostrils, it will forget its old conditioning and change, it will then move! The right amount of smoke will cause it not simply to panic, but to move from its imaginary shackles of the past. It may then discover its freedom and so dance with delight. Your task as a leader is to start a fire so your people see the flames with their own eyes, smell the smoke with their own nostrils, and then freely move on, to delight in the new-found freedom God wants for them. The trick, however, is to light a fire without burning the tent down! This is a delicate operation! Too much heat will lead to panic and a stampede, and your people will move, but probably elsewhere and leave your tent in tatters![9]

The process of imparting vision to implement change – of lighting the fire so others see the flames and smell the smoke – is a delicate one. One of the best pieces of advice I received from Jim Graham, while working with him as a student pastor at Gold Hill Baptist Church in Buckinghamshire, was 'Don't rush something through the church in six weeks and then spend the next six months sorting out all the misunderstandings. It is better to spend six months getting the church on board and you will have saved six weeks!' As David Watson used to say, 'If you are going to move a piano from one side of the platform to the other, move it an inch a week!' The old adage certainly holds true with imparting vision and implementing change – 'Make haste slowly.'

*Leadership + ownership = fellowship*
If you want to implement change with the minimum of pain then

in summary the following steps are needed –

1. *Impart the vision*. Create a clear today and a clear tomorrow. Plant a visible stake in the ground.

2. *Explain the inevitability of change*. John F. Kennedy said, 'The one unchangeable certainly is that nothing is certain or unchangeable.' Change is here to stay and an inevitable part of life, even church-life, but people do need help to cope with change.

3. *Increase the climate of discontent*. Light a fire without burning the tent down. Lower resistance and raise expectations. Build a sense of urgency so that people question the status quo and ask 'What changes are needed to move on?'

4. *Involve the church*. The people you lead need to be alongside you, so involve them in the process of change. You are the leader and you need to lead, but your people are not dumb sheep who will follow you faithfully and blindly. They need to 'own' the vision, so that it is not just 'theirs' but also 'ours'. So involve your people in the decision-making.

5. *Identify the 'opinion-formers' and 'change-resistors'*. In any group of people there will always be those who are ready for change and those who will always resist it. The bell curve in Figure 3 illustrates the way in which an average group responds to change.

   A leader should focus their attention on the negative and open people. Spend time with them, ensuring that they have clearly understood the vision, answer their concerns and questions honestly. Get these key people to move to the positive side. Admittedly, some people and some churches are more changeable than others, some seem unchangeable, but don't give up. Do not get too discouraged by the resistors, who will probably vote against change whatever is done!

6. *Isolate the problems*. Face up fairly and squarely to the anticipated problems and come up with realistic solutions. Develop a migration path so that people can follow your lead. Leaders need to have their head in the air to sense God's vision, but they also need to have their feet on the ground to practically work out the nitty-gritty details and ensure that the vision is well and truly earthed in reality.

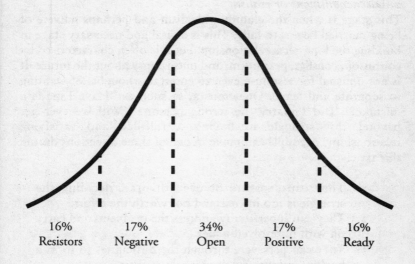

| 16% | 17% | 34% | 17% | 16% |
| Resistors | Negative | Open | Positive | Ready |

*Figure 3. The Bell Curve of Change*

### 4th leadership distinctive – a person of perseverance

Being a church leader can often seem like being married to the congregation! Some pastor's wives I know even refer to the demands of their congregation as 'the other woman'! Pursuing this analogy, it takes time to build trust and rapport into every marriage and likewise into church ministry. Perseverance and a commitment to make the relationship work are key factors. So every church leader, just like every couple contemplating marriage, will need to make adjustments and in so doing will normally experience three stages.

### 1. *Enchantment or romance*

At this initial stage a couple feel good about being together. Expectations are high and perhaps idealistic. They are optimistic about achieving their dreams. They are on honeymoon and have yet to truly discover each other, warts and all. This is but the beginning, for in every normal and healthy marriage there will inevitably be struggles.

## 2. Disenchantment or realism

This stage is when the glamour, idealism and perhaps naiveté of being married begins to fade. This is a vital and necessary stage in building the long-term relationship, but it is often characterised by confusion, conflict, pessimism, and uncertainty about the future. It is not unusual for a spouse even to entertain thoughts of wanting to separate and leave. Questions arise such as: 'Have I made a mistake?' 'Did I marry the wrong person?' 'Will we ever get beyond this struggle to having a fulfilled and satisfying relationship?' A couple can move in one of three directions during this time:

1. They can separate or even divorce, deciding the struggle is too intense and not worth the effort.
2. They can superficially address the problems and carry on with unresolved issues.
3. They can persevere through the difficulties to form a healthy, honest and deeper relationship.

The first two options, attractive as they might seem, will result in negative memories, unhealed hurts, self-doubts and an over-cautious approach to future relationships. The third option, although at times not always the easiest or even the most attractive, is the pathway to maturity.

## 3. Maturity or true relationship

This stage is the result of perseverance and results in long-term commitment. This is characterised by a deepening of the relationship, a sense of achievement, and a healthy perspective of one's self and others. Optimism and realistic expectations for the future are again part of the relationship. What is true for marriage is also true for ministry. There are times when a leader goes through the same stages and faces the same challenges as those of a newly-wed couple.

We need to recognise that although the leader's vision may be right, most visions may not be easily or quickly realised. People of vision need to become people of action, and action in turn involves hard work. This will undoubtedly involve overcoming obstacles from the world, the flesh and the devil; facing frustrations,

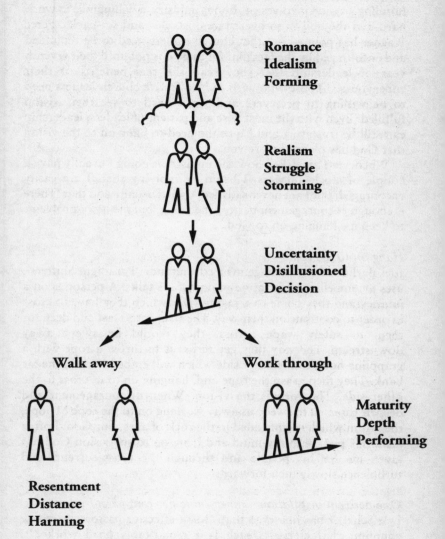

*Figure 4. Going the Distance*

disappointments, even faith-challenging setbacks. Make no mistake, fulfilling a vision involves enormous industry, a willingness to work hard and the ability to overcome obstacles and set-backs. Peter Wagner has pointed out that church leaders need to be reminded and encouraged by the fact that for most it is not until their seventh year of leadership that they reap the real benefits of their endeavours.[10] Those who wish to be effective church leaders need to be willing to persevere and work hard to see their vision fulfilled. Even with the most wise and patient of leaders, leadership can still be frustating and hence the need to hang on to the vision that God has placed before you.

Whenever I am asked how the ministry is going I usually have a couple of stock answers. I begin by replying that 'I am easily encouraged, but I am never satisfied.' I then usually add that 'There is enough encouragement to keep me going, but plenty of problems to keep me hanging on to God.'

## Hang on to the rope

Joel Barker of the management consultancy 'Paradigm Shifters', uses a compelling illustration in one of his talks. A person is on a journey and they come to a raging river which they have to cross in order to continue on their way. The river is too fast and deep for them to safely wade across, they would be swept away downstream. The way they get across is to throw a rope with a grappling hook to the other side which will embed itself in the far bank. They then grasp the rope and, hanging on to it, cross to the other side. The rope is the vision. When discouragement and despair threaten to sweep us away we hang on to the rope of hope, the vision which is embedded in the rock of ages, our God. I often have this picture in my mind and hang on to the vision God has given me for his people and through the cross-currents and turbulence slowly inch forward!

## One per cent inspiration – ninety-nine per cent perspiration

Lyle Schaller has observed that: 'Most effective pastors share one common characteristic: each is a remarkably hard worker.'[11] Fulfilling the vision is often one per cent inspiration and ninety-nine per cent perspiration. Moses discovered that a leader touched by God with the glow of the mountain-top experience does not remain there. God also sent him back down to experience the harsh realities of being in the valley with all its discouragements and disappointments (Exod. 32:18). An effective leader is one who can walk between the mountain-top and the valley, yet keeping their feet in place, their heart toward people and their eyes on God's vision.

## Vision + perseverance = faithful leadership

I will never forget the first two years as the senior pastor of Altrincham Baptist Church. There was many a time when I felt tempted to pack my bags and drive back down the M6! After the initial few months of honeymoon at the church there were many struggles to work through. At times it was sheer hard work. I was digging the foundations upon which I wanted to build. I was tilling the garden and planting the seed. It was not until my third and fourth years there that the results of my earlier labours bore fruit. I had to learn patience and perseverance. I had to learn how to build trust and faith in the church so that they felt confident to follow my lead. Those early days were challenging, sometimes discouraging and not always easy. I had to hold on to the belief that God had called me and that he had given me a vision of what he wanted to do. I would often say to myself that although the church was not what it could be, it was also not what it used to be, and it was not yet what it would be. I learnt much about myself and my God, and I thank him for the people and the privilege of calling me to minister among them.

By the time I moved on to my present church I could look back and see the hand of God on the church, and I regard my time at Altrincham as the most satisfying and fulfilling years of my ministry as a pastor.

## Entering the B zone

Ray and Anne Ortlund have made a study of Moses' leadership and analysed the phases of his ministry.[12] Moses responded reluctantly to God's call to set the Israelites free from Pharaoh. Yet having responded he then encountered great resistance from Pharaoh and had to overcome many problems, but through the plagues and the Red Sea, initial success was achieved. However, his problems had but begun! The catalogue of grumbling, rebellion and wandering

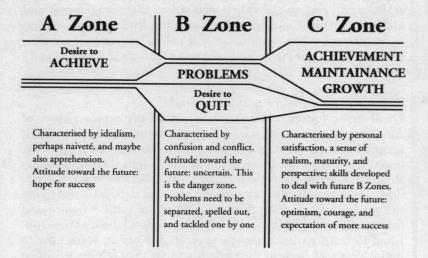

*Figure 5. Entering the B Zone[13]*

in the wilderness were constant challenges and discouragements to Moses. Many a time he found the task too great and wanted to quit. Eventually, however, success was achieved and the people entered into the Promised Land. The Ortlunds observe that Moses' ministry can be divided into three distinct phases: the A zone, the B zone and the C zone.

Most ministry situations start in the initial phase – the A zone. They soon hit the problem phase – the B zone where problems and people seem intractable. This is the danger zone, where a leader is tempted to quit the ministry or the church. The leader has to break through this into the achievement phase – the C zone. Beyond this phase a new A zone emerges and so the process continues. What was true for Moses was also true for Nehemiah, and is also true for every leader of God's people since. The A, B and C zones are not a once-for-all experience but a continual process through which mature ministry has to move constantly. For as every church leader knows, no church ever arrives or stands still – which is both an encouragement and a challenge!

It is vital to recognise when you are in the B zone. Perhaps this is where you are right now. You seem to be surrounded by nothing but problems. Your ministry seems to be characterised by the wounds, scars and self-doubts of battle. Perhaps you are tempted to step back, quit or even leave the fray. Take a moment to recall again the vision God imparted to you, a vision for you and your people. Recognise that by persevering and seeing it through, there can and will be a C zone. There can be a place of fulfilled vision, achievement and personal satisfaction. You will emerge with a renewed sense of realism, maturity and perspective on life. 'Being confident of this, that he who began a good work in you will carry it on to completion' (Phil. 1:6). God is able to bring both you and your people to the place he has planned and prepared for them.

The C zone is the place in which we all would want to be. What is more, it is the place that God also wants us to reach. Invariably, leaders discover that there is a B zone between the A and C zones! Between the inspiration of vision and success, there is the perspiration of struggle and perseverance. Yet with his help and grace at work in you and through you, you will be enabled to press on in your journey. You will be enabled to take the people you serve as leader, whom God has entrusted to your care, to move on and so fulfil the vision he has imparted to you.

*5th leadership distinctive – have a servant heart*

When I became the senior pastor of Altrincham Baptist Church in 1987 I moved from being a pastor at the Millmead Centre in Guildford. I left behind a modern purpose-built facility with a team of caretakers, and inherited an old Victorian building in dire need of attention and modernisation. We had no caretaker and the cleaning of the church was a rather haphazard arrangement. In those early months I can recall many occasions, late on a Friday afternoon, when I spent time cleaning the church toilets because they had not been done. At first I was resentful and felt it was beneath my calling to be doing such a thing. I rationalised that the church was paying me 'to devote myself to prayer and to the ministry of the word', to care for the spiritual needs of the congregation and community, not its basic physical needs. Through the experience, however, God had a lesson for me to learn!

## Toilet-training for the child of God

It was as if I could hear God ask me, as I swirled the brush around the pan, 'Didn't you come here to serve the needs of the people?' God needed to remind me of the call of all church leaders, which is to have a servant heart towards the people they seek to lead. After a year or so the church did appoint a caretaker and my toilet-cleaning ministry was taken from me, but I had learnt an invaluable lesson and I thank God for his practical training. Years before, I had visited Chuck Smith in Calvary Chapel, Costa Mesa, California, and he told me about his philosophy of ministry. One thing stuck in my mind. Their caretakers do not clean the church's toilets – that is the job of the student pastors. It is Chuck's belief that this life-lesson will instil into them, from day one, the importance of having a servant heart towards the people they serve. Having been toilet-trained myself – I thoroughly recommend it!

Effective leadership, as we have noticed, necessitates the use of several key skills. Simply to use these skills to influence people for your own ends, is to manipulate them to do what *you* want. Christian leadership, however, is about getting people to do what *God* wants. Christian leadership is a spiritual ministry which equips and edifies the church, which is the body of Christ. A leader's motive, therefore, is of paramount importance for they are not serving their own interests but God's. It is not only what they do that matters, but also why they are doing it. As we have pointed out, a generally accepted secular view of leadership is: 'Leaders engage in getting things done with and through people.' This is a helpful definition, but it is also an incomplete one. Christian leaders should be doing much more than that, for they are guiding people into doing what God wants. Effective leadership necessitates the use of several key skills to enable this to happen but a Christian leader is not seeking to serve their own interests but those of God.

Christian leaders are not simply managers but supremely ministers. In Christian leadership, the ends never justify the means. God calls his leaders to be servants, serving others and so serving the Master. Yet this genuine servant-style of leadership also knows the truth that a leader should be able to say to those they lead, 'I will be your servant, but I have only one Master!'

My father was a brigadier-general in the Army and I once asked him for his definition of leadership. He thought for a moment and then replied, 'Leadership is exercised when others wish to do what you would wish them to do.' To spiritualise his definition, 'Christian leadership is exercised when people wish to do what God wishes them to do.' This process calls for a genuine servant-style leadership. The paradox of a leader who does not lord it over their followers but seeks to serve them is a truth that lies at the heart of all effective leaders.

## Ministry not manipulation

In today's market-place there is much talk about power and position, about power-plays and takeovers. Christian leadership, however, is not about position, power, superiority, manipulation or tasks. It is about serving, ministry, people and relationships. I have discovered that people will follow a leader more enthusiastically when they consider their motives not to be self-serving. Yet, if we are honest with ourselves, we all serve with mixed motives and so we need constantly to check ourselves against the supreme example we have in the life of our leader – Jesus.

Any leader whose prime motivation is self-promotion and the desire for success to boost their own self-esteem is not following the example of Jesus. Yet, as the senior pastor of a church, I know that it is all too easy to fall into the trap of using people to fulfil my own projects and plans, to become task-orientated and not people-orientated. It is tempting as a leader to draw attention to yourself, to take all the credit and to declare, 'I did this!', 'Look what I've done!', instead of 'This is what we have done!' This attitude will quickly de-motivate people. Effective and secure leaders are quick to give praise, credit, encouragement and appreciation.

A leader's prime motivation should be to serve others, and not to serve their own interests and ambitions, however spiritual they may make them sound. Christ-centred leaders are driven, like the apostle Paul, by the love of Christ and a love for people (2 Cor. 5:14). Their heart is to serve God and his purposes which sees beyond the mere success of the project. People will follow those who genuinely have a servant-heart. Followers will forgive a great deal of their leader, if beyond seeing their feet of clay they also sense and feel a loving and serving heart. A servant attitude not only initiates and sustains the service of the Christian leader, it also provides the basis for their spiritual authority as the leader.

## Servant of all but serving only one master

In the early days of being a pastor at Altrincham Baptist Church I was attempting to explain my philosophy of ministry to the church meeting. I recall emphasising that I saw an important part of my calling was to minister to the needs of the congregation. In a response time it became clear that some people had interpreted that as meaning that I would be at their beck and call, that they could now tell me what needed doing and that I was duty bound to do it! In a moment of inspiration – or was it desperation? – the thought crossed my mind and almost without thinking I spoke out the phrase: 'I will be your servant, but I have only one Master.' Somehow that brought the right balance back into what I was trying to say. Since then I have often pondered that phrase myself and repeated it to others, for I believe it contains the biblical balance of a leader with a servant heart, serving Christ first and so serving others.

In my moments of frustration and discouragement, which I know all church leaders experience, when it seems as though my efforts and long hours have gone unnoticed, unrewarded or even been criticised, I have to remind myself of my true calling. God has called me to be a servant of the Master. I am working for him and he will reward me. If I lose sight of this, I find that I can quickly lose my servant-heart and I become resentful – even angry – with the response, complacency and comments of the congregation.

## In the ministry

Ordained clergy are often referred to as 'ministers', who are in 'the ministry'. Christians frequently speak of the work of the church as 'ministry'. What does the word literally mean? The word ministry comes from a Latin word *ministrare*, which means to help, to serve, to aid. It is the equivalent of the New Testament Greek word, *diakoneo*, from which we derive the word deacon, which means 'one who serves'. The word ministry, therefore, has at its very foundation the implication of serving others. So the next time someone refers to you as 'the minister', or being 'in the ministry', or you speak about 'my ministry', remember what it means! The very word is a constant reminder to you that God has called you, like Jesus, to be a leader with a servant heart.

Jesus said,

> You call me 'Teacher' and 'Lord', and rightly so, for that is what I am. Now that I, your Lord and Teacher, have washed your feet, you also should wash one another's feet. I have set you an example that you should do as I have done for you. I tell you the truth, no servant is greater than the one who sent him. (John 13: 13–16)

## 6th leadership distinctive – a consistent lifestyle

If you ask the average non-churchgoer why they do not go to church, they will throw out the usual theological issues such as 'suffering and a God of love', 'other world religions', 'evolution and creation', etc. Most church leaders are up on apologetics and so we comfortably and convincingly recite the standard answers. Near the top of most people's list, however, is another issue which is harder to explain away and which makes most leaders distinctly uncomfortable. It is crystallised by the likes of the American tele-evangelists, Jim and Tammie Bakker, Jimmie Swaggert and a host of other church leaders who have all fallen morally and made headlines in the Sunday tabloids. In recent years the British cabinet has been rocked by one revelation after another in the lives of so-called morally correct political leaders. Our non-churchgoer looks knowingly at us as if to infer that somehow all church leaders, when all the talk is said and done, are really no different – they just have not been caught! After all, they will argue, the Church is full of hypocrites and that certainly includes the leaders.

## Practice what you preach

For such sceptics, sadly, there is much evidence upon which they can build their case. It is, therefore, not surprising that leadership, in all arenas of life, is being scrutinised as never before. Today, the credibility of a leader is no longer assumed, but often has to be

proved. Christian leaders, it has to be admitted, are not always
Christ-like. There are many prices to be paid for being in leadership, and one of them has to be a willingness to be open, honest
and transparent before those you are called to lead. The effective
spiritual leader today is the one who can say, 'My life is an open
book, what questions do you have?' A leader's behaviour is crucial
as they seek to influence others and so change others' behaviour.

Leaders must practice what they preach. Despite the fact that
leaders may be put on a pedestal, the fact remains that we all have
feet of clay and that not one of us is perfect. Yes, leaders may
indeed even be placed on a pedestal only to be knocked off, yet,
nevertheless, you are called to be an example to those you lead.
Paul encouraged those he led to: 'Imitate me, as I imitate Christ'
(1 Thess. 1:6). In other words he didn't just 'talk the talk' but he
also 'walked the walk!' It is vital for you as a Christian leader that
your behaviour 'must be above reproach' (1 Tim. 3:2), and that you
'abstain from all appearance of evil' (1 Thess. 5:22).

### Money, sex and power!
It has been rightly said that 'the devil is not creative!' In other
words, his tricks and traps are as predictable and as old as the
Bible. Yet sadly, he does not have to be innovative. For example,
what worked with King David three thousand years ago has been
successfully employed countless times since with the leaders of
God's people.

I was recently involved in a Billy Graham mission and was
reminded of the strict standards and safeguards to which all the
members of the Billy Graham organisation adhere. Fifty years ago
they determined that they would not accept any money personally
for themselves from any mission. All money received goes towards
the cost of putting on the event and any surplus is used as seed-
money for the next mission. Billy Graham and members of his
team will not travel alone with any woman, apart from their wives,
no matter how short the journey. They have been vigilant in
guarding themselves against temptation and accusation so that the
gospel message may continue to be spread unhindered by innuendo
or scandal.

I was told the story of Muhammed Ali's visit to Billy Graham
some years ago. The boxer was expecting a chauffeur-driven

limousine to collect him at the airport, but was met instead by Billy Graham himself, dressed casually, driving a simple jeep. It is an interesting insight to know that Billy Graham has never owned any other type of car apart from a Ford! No wonder God's hand of blessing has remained on this man and his ministry for half a century – he truly practices what he preaches.

### Look but don't lust!

Let me address an issue that confronts every man. You notice a beautiful woman walking down the street. Somehow your eyes are inextricably drawn in her direction. You fight it but you give in. You remind yourself of what you have told others: that the first look is okay, it is the second look which is lust! You do feel, however, a little embarrassed and even guilty when she notices your look. Now that same beautiful woman is not at a distance walking down the street, but she is sitting across the room in your office. How do you handle the situation successfully and triumphantly? Here are three things that I remind myself in those situations.

First, I acknowledge the fact that the woman is beautiful! I recognise that women are one of the most beautiful aspects of God's creation. Like Adam, my breath can be taken away and I can thank God for the beauty of his creation.

Second, I remind myself that she is not mine to have. I can admire her but I cannot pursue her. I find it helps to contextualise both myself and her. In my office I have photographs of my wife and my sons. They remind me, and anybody else, of who I fully am and to whom I am committed. I will remind myself of the woman's family and so I will place her into her full and correct context. Temptation has a special power whenever anybody, particularly a Christian leader, isolates themselves, or the other person, from their full context.

Third, I pray for the woman's protection. I pray that God would preserve and protect her beauty. I pray that no one, including me, would misuse her lustfully and so rob and destroy her of her true inner beauty. These three simple keys have helped me as I have resisted the temptations of the evil one.

### Who pastors the pastor?

The questions that I think every Christian leader should ask of themselves are: 'Who pastors the pastor?', 'Who shepherds the shepherd?', 'Who counsels the counsellor?' Beyond your own self-discipline it is vital to have others who will commit themselves to stand alongside you. As a Christian leader you are vulnerable in so many ways. You are vulnerable to success, which can make you proud; to failure which can make you despondent; to discouragement and criticism which can make you depressed; to temptation which can make you fall. There are many fine people who would still be in the ministry today and who would not have fallen away if they had been surrounded by a supportive group of people with whom they could have been open and honest. Over the years I have discovered the importance of having such a group of people around me who will commit themselves to support me in my ministry.

### Be supported

My support group consists of four men whom I have chosen because of their friendship, integrity and willingness to encourage me and if necessary challenge me. They are all members of my church, but are not necessarily on the prime leadership team of the church. They see me in action and we talk frequently together informally. We meet formally on a monthly to bi-monthly basis. They will ask how I am doing personally and ministerially and will offer any feedback they may have observed. They will pray for me but they also have full permission to ask me the awkward question.

I have found my support group to be one of the most encouraging and constructive aspects of being a church leader. If I could wish and will anything into existence for you as a church leader, it would be that God would guide you to have a similar group of friends and confidants around you. The support and security it will offer to you, your family and your ministry I believe will be incalcuable.

There are those who will tell you that a church leader should not and indeed cannot form friendships with others in their church. This seems to be contradicted by Paul, not just with his teams but also with his congregations. His tender letter to the Philippians is a classic example. A leader is part of the body of Christ and so should enjoy its blessings. For someone to say otherwise seems to me to say more about themselves or perhaps their church. Both may need to be changed to a more biblical understanding of fellowship.

## Get off the pedestal!

A God-honouring, Christ-centred, consistent lifestyle is vital for the integrity of the Christian leader. It is vital that your talk and your walk are consistent with each other; that with God's help you are living up to the light that you have received and pass on to others. It is important, nevertheless, to remember that even as a leader, you are still a sinner saved by grace. You are still in the process of being perfected. Integrity does not mean upholding a pretence that you are without fault, that you never fail. Integrity is the commitment to not be a hypocrite, to not act out a part by saying one thing and yet be doing another.

Without constantly wearing your heart on your sleeve, or spilling your guts in public, it is good for Christian leaders to be vulnerable and transparent, to be willing to admit their mistakes and to acknowledge their faults. An openness even to being challenged and corrected by others is not only healthy, it is also biblical. No leader should ever be above contradiction or correction. You will discover that your honesty will be a source of encouragement and inspiration to those you lead as they hear you sharing honestly about personal and spiritual struggles. When this is coupled with a clear commitment to learn and to live a Christ-centred life, your honesty – rather than undermining your leadership – will actually enhance it. You will be seen as a fellow pilgrim, a fellow struggler who has learnt to find victory and freedom through Christ and so can truly help others. So do not place yourself on a pedestal! What is more, your honesty will also have the added bonus of preventing others from placing you on that pedestal from which you can only fall.

## 7th leadership distinctive – committed to team and to task

Ask anyone in Christian leadership and they will quickly tell you that there are just not enough hours in the day to do all that the Lord seems to want them to do! It is amazing that God actually had the time to be able to rest on the seventh day – the only explanation has to be that it was in the days before the creation of committee meetings! The expectations of their congregation and the demands of ministry, coupled with giving time for family, friends, recreation and personal space, promote too much stress and too much guilt for the average church leader. The result of all this is that many Christian leaders tend to fall into one of two extremes. They either become task-driven or people-driven. The tendency to become one or the other can be the result of many things – personality, circumstance, the tyranny of the urgent or listening to the person who shouts the loudest at the time!

## Types of leadership

Some leaders, because of the pressures to succeed and the need to get the job done, become project-driven and result-orientated. Their overriding concern is to achieve and to have an effective and efficient organisation. They rationalise that things must be managed well – to the glory of God! Their desire to achieve and the importance of getting the job done can, however, often obscure the needs of those doing the work. Being task-orientated can make them inspiring leaders from a distance, but a disappointment as a person when up close. People certainly know where they are going and they may have great respect for their leader. If they are brutally honest, however, they do not know him and may even not like him!

On the other hand, there are those leaders who in their eagerness to please people and to be available to them, never seem to get anywhere. The same issues are discussed year in and year out and promises are made to do such-and-such, yet all to no avail. Those who demand excellence of public ministry are often left frustrated as their harassed leader does his best with the limited time left at his disposal. Vision for the work and for the growth of the work is often no more than a dream at best, a nightmare at worst. Yet, because his people feel loved, a multitude of sins and shortcomings are forgiven as the group goes round and round in circles.

## A type or B type?

This dichotomy can also be a question of personality. Forty years ago two eminent cardiologists made a famous study of their patients and concluded that certain types were more likely to have a heart attack.[14] They divided people up into two broad groups – A type and B type personalities. The A type is the driver, the carnivore, the competitor, the go-ahead, go-get 'em workaholic, who has his finger in a number of pies, speaks quickly in short sentences, and who is a constant whirl of ideas, energy and activity. In contrast, the B type is the passenger, the herbivore, the participator, the meditator, member of the group, who has time to smell the roses and make small talk, who never seems overly busy and has time to stop and make time for everyone.

Christian leaders fall into both camps. Leaders who are task-orientated individuals are strong on vision, direction and determination, but are often correspondingly weak on building deep relationships and making people feel loved and affirmed. They are prone to driving themselves and their church into the ground and gaining a heart attack in the bargain! Leaders who are people-orientated make their members feel loved and needed. They produce a contented, caring church, but the church never grows or goes anywhere and so is weak in making a significant impact on its community. A general observation is that quite often larger churches tend to be led by leaders who have an A type personality and that frequently smaller churches tend to be led by leaders who have a B type personality. This is not always true of course, but it is very often the case.

## Task or people?

What type of leader are you? A number of resources have been developed to chart a person's tendency toward people or towards task. Most notable is the work of Robert Blake who devised the 'Leadership Grid' to test a person's orientation toward task or people. He has concluded that the best leaders are both proficient at initiating structure and showing consideration towards people.[15] Norman Shawchuck has devised a 'Leadership Styles Matrix' which incorporates additional leadership theory.[16] Based on their work I have designed the chart shown in Figure 6. Examine it and test your orientation toward task or people. Where would you place yourself? Are you more task-orientated or more people-orientated? Do you have a tendency to be in the top left-hand corner or to be in the bottom right-hand corner? The ideal balance is to be in the top right-hand corner.

You may operate in a certain way now, but I do not believe in a fixed, unchangeable personality. God can change you into being a more rounded and therefore more effective leader. Thank God for your strengths, but work on your weaknesses. The effective leader is the one who is both proficient at initiating and completing tasks and yet in the process shows consideration and care towards people.

There will always be a tension between completing the work/growing the kingdom and caring for the workers/others personal growth. Some leaders can fall into extremes: of being so task-orientated that relationships are overridden; or so relationship-orientated that their group neglects to achieve anything. Effective leaders balance their commitment to getting the job done with

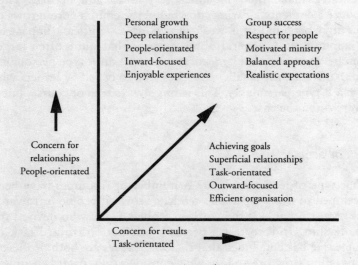

*Figure 6. People- or Task-Orientated?*

deepening the relationships within the body of Christ. No church or Christian group will ever have perfect relationships this side of the Rapture. Some churches or groups can go in ever-decreasing circles as all their time and energy is spent on building right relationships and helping members to find themselves and their place. The means of ministry has become an end in itself and, in looking inward, they have lost sight of their broader vision and mission.

Christian leaders are continually faced with the seemingly unresolvable tension between moving the work forward and caring for those doing the work; between completing the project and caring for the people. The effective leader is the one who can exert an encouraging and persistent influence to keep others moving towards the goal, yet at the same time not losing sight of the individual concerns of those who work with him. One of the goals of leadership is to have an effective ministry through having fulfilled people. It is true that when people feel good about themselves they come to expect more of themselves, which in turn creates a sense of confidence and high expectations in others and so the work is finished and the workers are fulfilled.

# 5

# Teammates

*Webster's Dictionary* cites the derivation of the word for team as coming from 'Two or more draft animals harnessed to the same vehicle or implement'.[1] The picture conjures up a team of oxen yoked to a plough. It is obvious to state that their purpose for being together is to plough. People may find themselves in a team and be left to wonder what they are supposed to be doing. They may end up ploughing a lone furrow, instead of being harnessed together with others towards a common purpose. Members of a team do fulfil different tasks, yet they should all be pulling in the same direction.

## Ploughing the same furrow

I have visited Israel often and have frequently watched a farmer ploughing with a team of oxen. The conclusion I quickly came to was that it is hard work to keep the team moving in the same direction! The oxen have a natural tendency to pull in different directions and it takes constant vigilance and cajoling from the farmer to keep them ploughing a straight furrow.

So it is with team ministry! It does not happen easily or naturally. Some team members can be very bullish in their approach to people. Others can be as stubborn as a mule. Some like to chew the cud. There are those who constantly chafe against the yoke. Some leaders like to crack the whip, whilst others hang on to the plough for dear life as the team drags them off in a new direction! There are several vital ingredients that will keep a team working together. First and foremost is to ensure that you are all pulling in the same direction.

The vision or direction of our current pastoral team is expressed as follows:

The pastoral team of Bramalea Baptist Church seeks to serve Christ, to be rooted in his Word, to be led by his Spirit and so to build the kingdom of God. They seek to minister with a servant-heart as they involve themselves in ministry and give oversight to church ministries. They will be accountable to the church board and to the church membership for the following responsibilities:

1. Implementing the church mission and vision statements
2. Overseeing specific church team ministries
3. Planning long-term and short-term strategies of ministry
4. Evaluating present and encouraging new church ministries
5. Reviewing and monitoring Sunday services and programs
6. Formulating pastoral policy to deal with pastoral issues
7. Ensuring healthy and honest team relationships
8. Exemplifying a Christ-like life and witness
9. Ministering to the church members, the body of Christ
10. Equipping the saints for the work of ministry

## Twelve-step approach to successful teams

The phrase team ministry contains two very important concepts: first, the notion of being a team; and second that of ministry. The implication is that a group of people have come together so that they can be more effective in ministering to others. The word ministry simply means an act of service, so ministry is the act of serving God by serving people. In team ministry, each member has not only been called by God to serve with their unique contribution, but they have also been called by God to serve alongside others in a corporate venture. Keeping the balance between commitment to the individual and commitment to the team is not always easy. Over the years, on the anvil of experience, I have hammered out a 'twelve-step approach' for successful team ministry. I believe these twelve principles, practically and consistently applied, will ensure that all the members of a team will plough the same furrow.

## Step 1. Unity, not uniformity

It is a remarkable scientific fact that for all the snow in the world, no two snowflakes crystallise in the same six-point formation. Each snowflake is unique. For all the grass in the world, each blade of grass has a unique pattern on its surface. What is true of nature is also true of human beings. I am an identical twin. My twin brother and myself look very alike, we have as close a genetic make-up as it is possible to have with another person. Yet we have a unique distinction – our fingerprints are not the same. No two people, however identical they may appear to be, have the same set of fingerprints. Scientists now tell us that the shape of a person's earlobe is yet another unique distinguishing feature!

God is not in the mass production business. Each person is a unique individual. When God's finger touches a life he does something wonderfully unique. When God's finger touches a team, or a church, or a partnership, and those people turn their ears to hear his voice, then God will do a unique work among them. A team is a unique grouping of unique individuals. Allowing for this uniqueness, there must be a unity which does not impose a uniformity.

### Unity
Larry Osborne, in his book *The Unity Factor* maintains:

> Unity is a vague term. While we easily recognize its presence or absence, few of us have spelled out carefully its essential elements. . . . there are 'three irreducible components' to unity:

1. Doctrinal Purity: agreement on our church's statement of faith does not mean theological uniformity.
2. Sincere and Warm Friendships: camaraderie built around genuine appreciation and respect for one another.
3. Philosophical Purity: basic agreement on priorities and methods, 'playing off the same sheet of music'.[2]

Unity means that a team is agreed on its vision, its purpose of ministry and philosophy of ministry. The team members present a united front on the fundamental approaches to ministry. Ensuing decisions, made by consensus, must be supported and endorsed by the whole team. There can be no gaps in the fence through which the enemy can crawl and create havoc in the backyard. Unity means that disagreement is allowed, even encouraged, during the discussion process. However, when a group reaches a decision, the dissonant voice must be stilled. What was debated behind closed doors must now be let go and not discussed in the market-place. The effective team needs to shine with a single beam of light, and not be refracted in a dozen directions. Individualism in a team is always to be applauded. An individualistic attitude in a team member, however, is a destructive element which must be avoided and, if necessary, challenged.

*Uniformity*
Team or group unity does not imply that there must be uniformity of team members. Uniformity imposes a sameness on each team member where there is no room for divergence. This can lead to unrealistic expectations being placed on others. Rick Warren helpfully and practically observes that in a team:

1. Do not expect every staff member to work at the same energy level all the time.
2. Be aware of external drains of energy on other staff members, and compensate for that.[3]

Every team or group needs to acknowledge that everyone does not have the same energy levels; cannot sustain the same level of output; does not have the same capacity for long hours or the ability to shoulder heavy workloads. People are not only different, but fluctuate in their capacity for their workloads and work intensity.

Uniformity seeks to eliminate variance of attitudes and beliefs; expression of opinions; lively discussion; even heated debate. Uniformity does not allow for different dress-codes, variety of temperament and personality, experiences of God and expressions of worship. Uniformity makes for a drab monochrome group. A group of people working together can be a glorious splash of technicolor. A team is not a group of genetic clones but God-gifted unique individuals pulling together. It is important for a team to distinguish between unity and uniformity. The former must be held on to at all costs; the latter must be avoided at all times.

## Step 2. Principle or preference?

One of the most vital ways to maintain a team's unity is to differentiate a principle from a preference.

### Principle

A principle is a fundamental tenet of belief. It may be a doctrinal viewpoint; a philosophical understanding of ministry; or a moral/ ethical framework of conduct or behaviour. If the group or team contravenes a principle held by a member, then the group must address the issue head-on and deal with the consequences. Violating a principle is a serious matter and the group either changes its decision, or the member should resign and leave. A principle is a deeply held cardinal belief which, if violated, would place the team, or a team member's place on the team, in serious jeopardy. It is extremely rare, however, for team decisions and disagreements to involve matters of principle. In most instances a person, beyond all the rhetoric, unswervingly goes out on a limb for a personal preference when it is not a principle.

### Preference

Preferences are often felt to be principles whereas in actual fact they are simply no more than personal opinions. Some people when working with others find it hard to change their own style and approach to ministry. They view their approach as the only right way. Other people feel they must win every argument. They struggle with not always getting their own way. Their insecurities propel them to the false conclusion that their opinion or their way of doing ministry must be right and others must share it. They have not learned to 'defer to one another in love', to learn from others, to have a submissive spirit, to respect other people's opinions/ preferences as equally valid. Sadly, some team members will go to the wall for a preference, convinced that it is a life or death principle.

When a person expresses their viewpoint in an intractable, prolonged or forceful way, I will ask them, 'Is this a principle or a preference?' The person is then challenged with the real issue. The point is made and they can gracefully back off. As the senior pastor and leader of the pastoral team I like to get my own way! When an issue is before us and my viewpoint is not winning the day, I will ask myself, 'Is this a principle or a preference?' Rarely is it a principle. So, if it is a matter which is not under my direct responsibility, I will argue my cause as cogently as I can and try to persuade others of my viewpoint. Having had my say, I have learned to leave it there and not to be offended or upset if my preference is not shared by everyone else.

### Step 3. Communication or consultation?

One of the areas that needs to be resolved early in the life of a team is the definition of precise boundaries of freedom and feedback that each team member has been given. The areas of empowerment and delegation have to be clearly worked through and spelled out. In our pastoral team we have established two boundaries: first, those areas in which a team member is allowed to make decisions unilaterally and then inform the team or team leader; and second, those areas in which the team member has to involve the team or team leader in the decision-making process. I refer to this distinction as 'communication or consultation'. We will use the phrase at our pastoral team meetings and leadership meetings to clarify what we are doing.

## Communication

Communication is when the individual team member has been delegated with the authority to make decisions within their area of responsibility. These decisions are then simply communicated back to the team. Communication is merely for information and clarification purposes only and not for discussion.

## Consultation

Consultation is when the team/team leader needs to be involved in the discussion and decision-making process. The team member therefore has to consult with them prior to any decision being made. These are the areas in which they are not empowered to make unilateral decisions.

The simple phrase 'communication or consultation?' has helped us give each other the necessary freedom to exercise leadership in our different areas of responsibility. It has also curtailed any unnecessary 'surprises' which may effect the whole team. This distinction helps us to underline once again our commitment to individualism, while avoiding the individualistic approach to team ministry.

## Step 4. Assertive but not aggressive

A good team is made up of gifted people who seek to bring out the best in each other; people who recognise, in the words of Ken Blanchard, that 'None of us is as smart as all of us.' Leadership teams, particularly the team leader, should therefore not be afraid of the gifts and strengths present in others that work alongside them. Leaders should be willing to receive the valuable input of others. A leadership team, however, by definition is usually made up of leaders. Those of us in leadership know only too well that as leaders we can tend to be forceful, dominant, even opinionated at times, as we seek to implement our vision, views and ideas. This can lead to creative tension! I have found it helpful to distinguish between being aggressive and being assertive.

## Don't be aggressive

Aggression is behaviour which seeks to dominate others. It forces the wishes of one person on to others. In the process it usually ignores the needs, wants, opinions and feelings of other people involved. Aggression is basically selfish because it puts ourselves first, and all others second. Through forceful behaviour we intimidate others into silence and and manipulate them into acquiescence.

## Don't be passive

The opposite of aggression is passivity. There are those who will not say what they think in a group and their silence is often mistaken for agreement. A passive person needs to learn, not how to be aggressive, but how to be assertive. You need to learn how to stand up for your ideas, feelings and gifts without standing on anyone else. You need to recognise that humility does not mean being a human doormat. You need to be courageous and learn how to share your feelings and voice your opinions.

## Be assertive

Between the extremes of aggression and passivity is assertion. Assertiveness has been defined in the following way:

> Assertion involves standing up for personal rights and expressing thoughts, feelings and beliefs in direct, honest and appropriate ways which do not violate another person's rights. . . . The basic message in assertion is: This is what I think. This is what I feel. This is how I see the situation. The message is expressed without dominating, humiliating or degrading the other person. . . . Assertiveness involves respect – not deference – respect for oneself as well as respect of the other(s).[4]

Being assertive is the willingness to state your case strongly without denying the rights of others. It is rooted in the belief that we all have a valuable contribution to make to the discussion and decision. It is important that you clearly state your ideas, wishes or views, but in such a way that others may hear and take account of your position. It is equally important that you also encourage others present to state their ideas and views. A good leadership team dynamic is when people feel free to communicate openly, clearly and sensitively. Each person present is encouraged to assert themselves and help others to do the same. In this way, every person, not just a vocal few, has the opportunity to state their views. The group demonstrates the freedom in allowing varying views to be expressed and so truly discern what God may be saying through all present. This freedom of exchange will enhance the creativity of the group, the ownership of the decisions that are made, and possibly the wisdom to discern what the Lord may truly be saying.

## Step 5. Keep short to stay sharp

Even with the best will and intentions in the world, misunderstandings, miscommunication, wrong words and even wounds will inevitably happen in the life of every lively and healthy team. Let's be realistic, even people who love one another dearly, as in marriages and families, sometimes say and do the most thoughtless things at times. The question is not, 'How to avoid them?' but, 'How to handle them when they happen!' In a later chapter we will explore the whole area of how a team should handle and resolve conflict. Sufficient to say at this point, that a team should convey the ethos of being 'short to be sharp'.

### Keep short accounts
A group of people that is committed to keeping short accounts with the Lord and with one another is going to stay healthy and together. What is more they will maintain their sharp cutting edge in ministry. In my experience, too many people working together sweep matters under the carpet, leaving situations and hurts unresolved. This does not mean that a person should dig up every little incident from the past. It does mean honest reflection back to a person if you have been hurt or wounded by what they may have said or done. The writer of the Hebrews warns, 'See to it that no one misses the grace of God and that no bitter root grows up to cause trouble and defile many' (Heb. 12:15).

A sign of healthy relationships is when those who work closely together feel that they have the freedom to approach one another and share those times when things may have gone wrong. I have discovered that it is often in the honesty of those moments that people are drawn even closer together. A person reflects their hurt, or recounts the misunderstanding in a situation. The other recognises their insensitivity. Tears may be shed. An apology, forgiveness and reconciliation soon flow.

## Stay spiritually sharp

Keeping short accounts means we keep our spiritual sharpness. The following attitudes all indicate an underlying malaise: hanging on to incidents from the past; harbouring grudges; recounting grievances; remembering the mistakes of others; strained relationships; emotional or physical distancing. The result, in most cases, is that the person, sometimes even the entire team, opens the door and gives the devil a foothold right inside the leadership camp. It can hardly be a surprise that the team loses its spiritual cutting edge and sharpness in ministry. So team members should remember the maxim and be encouraged to 'Keep short accounts, in order to stay spiritually sharp!'

## Step 6. Critique and not criticise

Not one of us is perfect and so there will always be plenty of room for improvement. One of the key ways to become more Christ-like is to be open to feedback from those with whom we work closely. The Scriptures teach 'As iron sharpens iron, so one [person] sharpens another' (Prov. 27:17). Yet sometimes in the process the sparks can fly! God, nevertheless, wants to use those around you to sharpen your spiritual cutting edge, to remove those rough spots and so make you a more effective tool in his hands.

In a team it is, therefore, important to be open to feedback from others – in fact you should positively invite it from others. It is vital, however, that the feedback that is given is the right kind, that it is constructive and not destructive. I draw the distinction between being criticised and being critiqued.

## Criticism

Criticism is negative, destructive and is focused on fault-finding. It often leaves a person feeling condemned and destroyed. Criticism is problem-orientated and concentrates on the narrow band of a person's weaknesses and faults and so loses sight of the total person, which also includes their strengths. Criticising can become a way of life for some people who make a habit of putting others down. We speak of those who have a critical spirit, for whom, whatever the reason, criticising others has become an addictive pattern of behaviour. This may enhance their own image and bolster their insecurity by bringing others down, but it can be devastating in the close quarters of a team set-up.

Criticism is destructive because it often comes across in an unloving manner which undermines a person rather than builds them up. People do take things personally! So it is not okay to point out someone else's problem and then walk away leaving them in pieces. Feedback without love and hope is criticism, which at best is unhelpful and at worst is devastating.

## Critique

To critique someone is to be positive, constructive and focused on them as a total person. It takes a broad view of the person which acknowledges their strengths and not just their weaknesses. Good feedback begins with a person's strengths and then moves to some (not all) of their weaknesses. It looks for ways to help them work through their problems or blind spots. It seeks to build up the person through exploring possible ways of helping them to strengthen their weaknesses. It is not satisfied with simply drawing attention to what a person is doing, but is also concerned as to why a person may be reacting in a certain way.

In other words to critique someone is to look at the total picture. It does require more patience, time and effort, but in that way the person is really sharpened by you and not just hit by you! So the next time you give (or receive) feedback, ask yourself the question, 'Was I critiquing or criticising?'

## Step 7. Gifted but teachable

Peter Drucker rightly observes that a team needs to have confidence in every team member's ability to perform by having the 'essential ingredient for teamwork: mutual respect'.[5] It is axiomatic that each team member is uniquely gifted by God and thus has a unique contribution to make to the total team effort. The team should celebrate the gifting that God has given them in each other. They should be quick to affirm those gifts, both in private and in public.

No one, however, has arrived. There is always room for improvement. The quality and effectiveness of a person's gift can and should be ever-increasing. A team can be a tremendous tool in the hand of the Lord to hone up a person's gifts and skills for ministry. There is no better way to continue to learn than in the context of supportive fellow teammates, who know us, are cheering for us and want the best for us and from us.

One of the key evangelical leaders of today is undoubtedly John Stott. When I became a Christian, in the early 1970s, his church at All Souls, Langham Place in London, became my first spiritual home. Over the years I continue to appreciate his ministry and insights. One of the members of the pastoral team at Altrincham Baptist Church worked at All Souls for three years. At his first ministry team meeting at that church, John Stott, as was his custom, asked all those present to critique his Sunday message! My friend was impressed that a man with a worldwide ministry, nevertheless, still demonstrated a humble and teachable spirit.

I have had the opportunity to view the pastors at Willow Creek Community Church at close hand and have observed a similar teachable spirit. They have a 'commitment to excellence', modelled by the senior pastor Bill Hybels. This has produced an openness to feedback in those who work there. Indeed, what has impressed me is that it is a positive seeking out of feedback. This attitude pervades their ministry and constantly fuels the desire to continue to improve the gifts that God has entrusted to them.

A teachable spirit is borne out of a secure sense of God's gifting and acceptance. Insecure people struggle with receiving any negative feedback from others. I have been astounded at how many insecure people end up in the Christian ministry, and so on many pastoral teams and missionary stations! I have discovered that an insecure person who receives nine positive comments and one negative comment, will only remember the negative one! The person will probably also accuse you of being critical, discouraging and non-affirming! Their defensive reaction is simply a classic smoke-screen to cover their own insecurity. The temptation is to back off and avoid critiquing them or their ministry. The right approach, however, is patience, persistence and bags of encouragement, and at the same time, addressing and working through the deeper issues with them. A teachable team is a healthy team. It mirrors to those they lead that we are all in the learning process.

## Step 8. Authority and accountability

It is vital that team members feel that they have been given the authority to carry out their responsibilities. They have been trusted with their ministry responsibilities. Trust has to be both given to people and earned by them. A person is, in all probability, on the team because they have shown evidence of ability and gifting which has been recognised by others. There is a foundation of confidence in what God can do through them already in place. A person must be held accountable for the authority which has been entrusted to them.

I recall a team member who, whenever he was asked to report back and update me on the progress of his projects and responsibilities, would say somewhat disarmingly to me, 'What's the matter, don't you trust me?' Initially, this ploy caught me off guard and I did not pursue it. I quickly learned, however, that this was his subtle way of avoiding the issue of accountability. It became very apparent that he was not producing the goods, hence his resistance at being held accountable to anyone for what he did, or did not do.

All team members need to be accountable; initially to the leader; mutually to each other; ultimately perhaps to a leadership board, church meeting or whatever. Accountability does not imply lack of trust. It allows the opportunity for honest appraisal, loving reflection and so, hopefully, reinforcement of that which has been entrusted individually to a team member or collectively to a team.

Rising up from the foundation of trust a team member must build with two essential materials: first, consistency, and second, loyalty. These take time to construct. In the initial phase of team building, the team leader is looking for the confirming signs of a consistent, persistent, level output and quality of ministry. Whilst recognising that everyone works in energy bursts, there does need to be consistent output.

If a team member's ministry, however, is consistently characterised by fits and starts; highs and lows; being hot and cold; workaholism and weariness; then they lack the quality of consistency. In the long run this will undermine the trust that the leader and others feel confident to place in them. If a person begins a project, but does not complete it; or draws up plans, gets them approved, but then does not implement them; then they have a problem with consistency which they need to face and work through.

Loyalty is a vital building block in the process of increasing trust. Inevitably in every team there are things that are said and done which may not concur with every team member's preferences. The key test is the way in which a person handles those situations. Lack of loyalty to the team's discussions and decisions will erode trust faster than almost anything else. Talking down the team or team leader will make them and others very wary of investing increasing trust in that person.

## Step 9. Delegation without abdication

Inevitably, in every team somewhere along the line the ball gets dropped, an assignment gets blown. This can lead to frustration and recrimination. It is, therefore, vital to underscore the management adage which states that, 'You can delegate authority but you can never abdicate responsibility.' In pastoral teams each team member is given responsibility for different areas of the life of a church. In fulfilling those responsibilities each team member needs to enlist the help of a host of volunteers to get the job done. In the process they will recruit others to take on specific functions. The management term for this is 'empowerment'.

> 'Empower' means to give power or authority, to enable or
> give ability . . . Empowerment refers to the process whereby
> an organization enables or encourages all individuals to
> more fully participate by giving them greater freedom,
> responsibility, and decision-making authority – by enabling or
> encouraging them to more fully exercise their inherent power.
> Empowerment taps into and unleashes the full potential in an
> individual and in an organization.[6]

It is not only appropriate but vital for team members to release
others into ministry and so broaden the base of involvement and
leadership. The biblical mandate for those on a pastoral team is not
to do all the ministry. It is 'to prepare God's people for works of
service' (Eph. 4:12); or 'to equip the saints for the work of
ministry' (RSV). Frustration, however, can creep into the running
of a team if a member, under the plausible guise of 'empowering'
others or – to use Frank Tillapaugh's phrase, 'unleashing'[7] others –
is clearly abdicating their responsibility. Delegation of authority to
another never entails the abdication of your responsibility. You
may delegate authority to a person to do something, but you will
always retain the responsibility for how they perform the task
you have given them. You can never abdicate your leadership
responsibility.

President Harry Truman's desk plaque, 'The buck stops here' is
true for everyone who has been entrusted with a position of
leadership and its accompanying responsibility. Team members
usually have their own specific areas of responsibility. It is vital that
you also constantly mentor and monitor those to whom you have
given authority. In the final analysis, you cannot wash your hands
of that responsibility. You cannot claim ignorance, nor maintain,
'I've been let down.' As the person at the top, you will rightly
always be held responsible for what happens under you. After all,
you are the one who chooses what to assign and to whom to assign
it. It is therefore not unreasonable that you should also be the
person who should be held accountable for the consequences of
those to whom you choose to delegate authority and so to
'empower' or 'unleash' into ministry.

*Step 10. Encouragement and exhortation*

Over the years I have been particularly blessed by those individuals who have taken the time to write a letter or who have penned a few lines inside a card. Their words of encouragement, appreciation or affirmation have often been a ray of sunshine. God's timing never ceases to amaze me. Frequently an encouraging word arrived at the right moment. We all need encouragement to keep us going, to make us feel that what we are doing is worthwhile. Encouragement lifts the spirit and can make a world of difference to a person's self-esteem and workload. It is extraordinary what a difference it makes when our efforts are noticed. It is a real boost to know that someone has taken the time and made the effort to tell us we are appreciated. I wonder how much you know about Joseph, the Levite from Cyprus? Perhaps more than you might at first think! He was known in the book of Acts by his Aramaic nickname, 'Son of Encouragement', that is Barnabas. What a difference he made in the lives of Saul/Paul, John Mark and those early church team ministries.

One of the encouraging things that a leader, and indeed a team member, can do is, using Tom Peters' phrase, to 'Manage by walking about'.[8] In other words, take time to drop in on another's ministry or activities, if only for a few minutes. It demonstrates your interest in them and your encouragement of their ministry. Your time will be well spent and much appreciated. In the understandable hustle and bustle of team ministry it is all too easy to take teammates for granted. When this is coupled with the fact that there is an uncanny aspect of human nature which has a tendency to focus on the dark side, the negative, to spot the mistake, to notice the missed assignment, the need for positive encouragement is all the more essential.

People are quick to notice when things are not going well, or when allocated tasks have not been fulfilled adequately. We all have our blind spots and others, whom we allow to get close to us, usually see them straight away. We have already noticed how important it is to exhort people, to challenge people, to hold others 'to the highest', at times even to confront people. If these are not done in the consistent framework and atmosphere of an encouraging environment, then our admonishments will fall on deaf ears and hardened hearts. We need to be known as those who notice the white as well as the black, who spot the good as well as the bad. Well-intentioned exhortation without accompanying encouragement, even among secure individuals, will hinder rather than help that person to see their blind spots and overcome their obstacles to personal growth.

Rick Warren says that helpful terminology can diffuse those times in a team when situations have gone wrong and need to be addressed and corrected. He says that the aftermath should be referred to as, 'the management of mistakes'. The emphasis, rather than being the ethos of a post-mortem, should be, 'mistakes are useful, for they teach us what doesn't work.'[9]

### Give credit where credit is due

Another important aspect of affirmation is that of giving proper recognition to team members, not only in private but also in public – to give credit where credit is due. Public praise and appreciation of each other's ministries solidifies teamness and increases team spirit.

Several years ago I worked with a team leader and shared with him a great idea that I had devised for encouraging the congregation to get involved in ministry. I came up with a creative brochure and a snappy title. The team leader suggested that he should go away and work on the idea and then present it to the congregation. I readily agreed. When he spoke to the congregation and informed them that, 'I have come up with this great idea!' I thought he was joking. I quickly realised he was not! He simply wanted to take the credit for himself. I approached him on the matter afterwards and he retorted, 'Well, what does it matter whose idea it was, as long as the people get it?' It seemed so reasonable, and I was made to feel self-seeking. Unfortunately, this credit-taking was not a one-off example. It slowly undermined the credibility of our relationship. I have learned from that experience.

I endeavour to be quick to give credit to other team members, to celebrate their successes, to consistently praise them in public and in private. I thus hope to keep them both motivated and appreciated.

## Step 11. Strong and sweet

When I became the senior pastor of a particular church, one of the deacons took me aside and told me that the leadership team there was a strong one. He warned me that they were not 'yes men'. I replied, 'Great, I am not threatened by that. I welcome strong leaders around me.' Some team leaders prefer a group of assistants below them, who clearly look up to them as leader. I prefer a group of associates around me who look to me as their leader. This distinction is an important one.

It has to be realised that strong players, with all their talent and ability, can also be very single-minded and strong-willed. I never have a problem with things being said strongly, provided that they are also said with grace! One of the statements made of Jesus by John, was that Jesus was full of 'grace and truth' (John 1:14). My observation of working closely with others, is that some people can be so full of truth that they lack grace. They are so sure they are right, that they treat others wrongly. Thinking we know the truth is never an excuse to be lacking in grace. No matter how certain a person may be of the spiritual rightness of their viewpoint, it is unspiritual and wrong to neglect to heed Paul's admonition to 'speak the truth in love' (Eph. 4:15).

No matter how spiritually compelling a person's opinion or concern may appear, it will, in reality, be 'only a resounding gong or a clashing cymbal' unless it is given with grace and spoken in love (1 Cor. 13:1). To put it in today's idiom: it is okay to be assertive, provided that you are not obnoxious! It is okay to disagree, but do not be disagreeable! It is okay to point things out, but not to point the finger! I encourage people to be full of truth, but I will also challenge them to be full of grace. Team members need to be strong and sweet!

## Step 12. Meeting for ministry

For any team to function well there needs to be good working relationships. It is crucial that the team and its members are committed to meeting regularly. This should be viewed as an essential top priority commitment. Some team members tend to view it at best as important but not essential, at worst as an additional burden. Their sporadic attendance may reflect those attitudes. The importance of the meetings must be spelled out. The meetings should be made relevant to all those present; not be boring; include discussion and not predominantly be a lecture from the leader.

Absenteeism may also be an indication that a team member is not 'in synch' with the team or has fallen out with a team member. Absenteeism may indicate a number of things, so it is crucial to learn what the cause may be in each case. It is vital to secure a clear commitment from all team members to attend the meeting. The meeting takes absolute precedence over all else, bar a major pastoral or personal need. In pastoral ministry, a full-time team should be meeting at least once every week. Part-time lay leadership teams should be meeting at least once a month, preferably once a fortnight. The purpose of meeting, beyond all else, is to enhance the team's effectiveness in ministry, hence its importance. The team is meeting for ministry.

The meetings will undoubtedly vary in content, depending on the agenda, but ought to be a wholesome mixture of several ingredients: business matters; practical details; ministry feedback; Sunday evaluation; communication and consultation issues; mutual encouragement; personal exhortation; relating socially; spiritual formation; seeking God; maintaining the vision. The meetings should include times of prayer, in which the team, as well as praying for others, should pray with each other. Modelling spiritual ministry within the team will enable the team to minister more comfortably and effectively outside of the team.

Our church leadership team meets once a fortnight; our pastoral team meets at least once a week. We use the different opportunities to focus on different aspects. Occasionally, we will set aside our regular meeting agenda and take off as a pastoral team and go ten-pin bowling or play golf, which humbles some of us but refreshes us all! I suggest regular team retreats, at least once or twice a year, for us all to get away from our familiar surroundings to give concentrated time to the never-ending process of team building.

## Staying yoked together

It is indeed hard work for a team of gifted individuals to plough the same furrow. Pulling together and remaining focused is a constant challenge. I have found that using the 'twelve-step approach' to team ministry gives guidelines which help to keep the team moving forward in the same direction. It keeps the team harnessed together, walking at the same pace, and ploughing a straight furrow. It enables them to look down the furrow into the distance. In so doing they will stay working closely together and remain ploughing in a true and straight line.

# 6

# Team formation

Each year in American professional sports, such as football, basketball, or baseball, there is D-Day: Draft Day. This is the most crucial day in the off-season calendar, for it is the day for the club to select the best available players and so secure the future health and prosperity of the team. The coaches have spent months scouting out the players who are not only the most talented on the field of play, but who are also the right fit for the team. In this way the team hopefully will have strength and depth in all aspects of its game and so be a balanced team. In the context of spiritual ministry, what are the qualities that a team leader should be looking for when considering adding new team members to a team?

## Team building

If you have the choice, it is surely ideal to have those people working alongside you with whom you naturally relate well. To put it simply, if you are in the enviable position of being able to pick your own team, pick people you like! I have come across teams, however, whose members were chosen simply because they were people the senior pastor had come to know and like. They were a great relational fit, but the ministry fit was appalling. The result was that the team was ineffective, its members frustrated in ministry, and so inevitably their relationships became strained. The team, needless to say, had a rapid turnover of staff.

## Ministry fit and relational fit

Don Cousins, the former associate pastor at Willow Creek Community Church, maintains that to select the right players the following four essential elements should be explored:

1. Strength of character.
2. Spiritual authenticity.
3. Ministry fit.
4. Relational fit.[1]

Their 'ministry fit' means that people are doing that which reflects their spiritual gifts, spiritual passion, talents, personality, temperament and background. Their 'relational fit' means that team members must like one another, enjoy working with another, benefit from each other, work well together and have the right chemistry.

It is vital to take both ministry fit and relational fit together when forming a team. Both ingredients are crucial if a team is to work well and be successful. Ministry fit will obviously be determined by the context of ministry and the job description for their particular role on the team. This will probably remain reasonably fixed for the person's duration on the team. Relational fit is determined by the person's character and may be much more variable as the person faces the challenges of ministry in general and team ministry in particular.

It is therefore vital to give quality time to process the potential relational fit of a person on to your team. Simply determining a person's academic credentials, although important, may not be as vital to a team in the long run, as accurately determining their character assessment. A collection of great individual all-stars can often be beaten by a great team of ordinary individuals who play well together.

Team building is 'the process of unifying a group of people with a common objective into an effectively functional team'.[2] The following areas need to be covered in the team building process:

1. There is a healthy balance between being task-orientated and relationship-orientated.
2. There is a recognition of who each member is; their

individual personalities, their strengths and weaknesses.

3. There is a willingness to recognise and face the process
   necessary in adjusting to becoming a team.
4. Team members accept their team role and responsibilities.
5. The team learns how to resolve differences that will
   inevitably occur.

## Moving in the right circles

John Adair, in his formative work on teams, describes three
'interlocking needs' of team life, which he represents by three
circles. Each of the elements in Adair's model (task, team,
individual) represent legitimate needs which the team has to meet.
Failure to do so will reduce the team's effectiveness. Adair suggests
that effective teams are those who are able to balance these
sometimes conflicting elements.

In the initial phase of team building, the team goes through an
individual-orientated phase, in which individual needs and
concerns predominate the agenda. Team members are seeking
answers to the questions: 'Who am I?' 'What are my gifts?' 'What
is my role?' This can be an unsettling time in the life-cycle of a
team as people find their place. Some groups never emerge from
this phase and it can continue to dominate their ongoing life. In
such groups individual needs dominate its life and navel-gazing,
manipulation, point-scoring and conflict are the order of the
day.

In the task-orientated phase, the members are seeking answers
to questions such as 'What can I do?' 'What is my responsibility?'
'What is my contribution?' Those teams which struggle with
building personal relationships in the initial individually orientated
phase, may adopt an avoidance strategy by throwing themselves
headlong into their task. Task-orientated groups are characterised
by high activity and low relationships. They focus on targets and
not people. The needs of the individual or the team are
subordinated and may even be sacrificed in order to achieve the
task.

*Figure 7. Interlocking Needs of a Team[3]*

Effective teams will always contain a creative tension within them. There has to be a healthy balance between relationships and task, between individuals and the team. Within the group, disagreement, challenge and hard questions are allowed, even encouraged. They are not viewed as threats to team unity because of the supportive and encouraging environment of the team. Feelings and views of others are respected, but open to challenge. In a mature team this will not lead to dissonance and disharmony but to increased creativity, progress and productivity.

The aim of building a healthy team is to focus on each phase when appropriate, and then to hold all three elements in balance. Many teams tend to stay stuck in the rut of being, in particular, relationship-orientated, task-orientated or team-orientated. There are times when it clearly is appropriate for a team to focus on one of the elements and it will naturally dominate the group. Over the long haul, however, there should be a creative balance of all three elements. The mature and healthy team has all three circles overlapping and equal in size.

*Knowing your teammates*

There are three vital keys to successfully working with others:

1. Know yourself.
2. Know others.
3. Know your God.

There are many different tools on the market today for assessing character/trait/temperament/personality. I have found the following useful in my ministry generally, and in discerning the relational fit of team members in particular.

'The Taylor-Johnson Temperament Analysis Profile' was initially devised by Roswell Johnson in 1941 and revised by Robert Taylor in 1967 and then again in 1984. It contrasts sixteen different character traits: Nervous—Composed; Depressive—Light-hearted; Active-social—Quiet; Expressive-responsive—Inhibited; Sympathetic—Indifferent; Subjective—Objective; Dominant—Submissive; Hostile—Tolerant; Self-disciplined—Impulsive. It is an excellent test which I use regularly in my ministry. It does require a certified person to administer it or the services of a professional consultant.

'The Myers-Briggs Type Indicator' is another well-known test, which is based on Carl Jung's work, *Psychological Types,* released in 1921. Jung's work was adapted by Isabel Briggs Myers in 1943, who maintained that people adopt four functions – the functions of Sensing (S), Intuition (N), Thinking (T) and Feeling (F) – which can also be coupled with four attitudes which are: the attitudes of Extrovert (E), Introvert (I), Judging (J) and Perceiving (P). The combination of all the above produces one of sixteen 'preference types' indicated by the respective letters. In some circles, team members are known by their 'preference type' initials! It is a very popular and comprehensive analysis, which requires a certified person or a professional consultation.

There are modified versions of these personality assessment tools available for general use. These are not as comprehensive and therefore arguably, not as accurate, but they still provide excellent insights into the make-up of a person, and so that of a fellow team member. The most helpful of these is *Please Understand Me* by David Keirsey and Marilyn Bates. Some regard this 1978 book as a landmark contribution. David Keirsey drew on over twenty years of experience in refining the work of Myers-Briggs. The book contains an excellent explanation and portrait of each type, as well as a shortened version of the full test and I would highly recommend it.

'*The Four Basic Temperaments*' was resurrected by Professor Hans Eysenck, a British psychologist, based on the ancient Greek belief of Hippocrates that there are four basic temperament types: (1) choleric, (2) sanguine, (3) melancholic and (4) phlegmatic. Eysenck propounded his theories on 'the dimensions of personality' through scientific articles in the 1950s and a eventually in a book, *Know Your Own Personality* in 1975. His views were popularised by Tim LaHaye with a series of books beginning with the bestseller *Spirit Controlled Temperament* in 1966. These 'four temperament types' have become well-known indicators of personality and have been used by a wide range of people. The approach, although seemingly over-simplified, is very helpful in gaining a quick, clear and reasonably accurate assessment of a person's behaviour patterns. They can be given to people who, somewhat subjectively, identify their strengths and weaknesses, and so establish their temperament mix. A person is never one type exclusively, but a blend of at least three.

'*Your Management Temperament Profile*' produced by Myron Rush is based on these temperament types and is an excellent team test. It is easy to administer but reasonably accurate in gaining a quick overview of the way a person acts with and reacts to others in a team. He groups people into four basic managerial types along the lines of the four basic temperaments:

A – Promotional – Sanguine.
B – Concept – Melancholic.
C – Operational – Choleric.
D – Negotiating – Phlegmatic.


*Criss-cross*

All these tests enable a person to own their weaknesses as well as know their strengths and have the initial advantage of being easy

## Table 4. 'Your Management Temperament Profile' Test

Name _____

*Rate yourself as to the extent the following characteristics represent you. Rate yourself on each characteristic with 10, most like you, 1, least like you.*

### A Score _____
#### 200

| | |
|---|---|
| Outgoing, Sociable | 1 2 3 4 5 6 7 8 9 10 |
| Inspires Allegiance | 1 2 3 4 5 6 7 8 9 10 |
| Sincere | 1 2 3 4 5 6 7 8 9 10 |
| Positive Attitude | 1 2 3 4 5 6 7 8 9 10 |
| Responsive to Others | 1 2 3 4 5 6 7 8 9 10 |
| Talkative | 1 2 3 4 5 6 7 8 9 10 |
| Enthusiastic | 1 2 3 4 5 6 7 8 9 10 |
| Seldom Worries | 1 2 3 4 5 6 7 8 9 10 |
| Compassionate | 1 2 3 4 5 6 7 8 9 10 |
| Generous | 1 2 3 4 5 6 7 8 9 10 |
| Undisciplined | 1 2 3 4 5 6 7 8 9 10 |
| Easily Influenced | 1 2 3 4 5 6 7 8 9 10 |
| Restless | 1 2 3 4 5 6 7 8 9 10 |
| Disorganised | 1 2 3 4 5 6 7 8 9 10 |
| Undependable | 1 2 3 4 5 6 7 8 9 10 |
| Loud | 1 2 3 4 5 6 7 8 9 10 |
| Promotes Self | 1 2 3 4 5 6 7 8 9 10 |
| Exaggerates | 1 2 3 4 5 6 7 8 9 10 |
| Fearful, Insecure | 1 2 3 4 5 6 7 8 9 10 |
| Unproductive | 1 2 3 4 5 6 7 8 9 10 |

### C Score _____
#### 200

| | |
|---|---|
| Determined | 1 2 3 4 5 6 7 8 9 10 |
| Independent | 1 2 3 4 5 6 7 8 9 10 |
| Productive | 1 2 3 4 5 6 7 8 9 10 |
| Decisive | 1 2 3 4 5 6 7 8 9 10 |
| Practical | 1 2 3 4 5 6 7 8 9 10 |
| Goal Oriented | 1 2 3 4 5 6 7 8 9 10 |
| Optimistic | 1 2 3 4 5 6 7 8 9 10 |
| Willing To Risk | 1 2 3 4 5 6 7 8 9 10 |
| Self-confident | 1 2 3 4 5 6 7 8 9 10 |
| Willing To Lead | 1 2 3 4 5 6 7 8 9 10 |
| Unsympathetic | 1 2 3 4 5 6 7 8 9 10 |
| Inconsiderate | 1 2 3 4 5 6 7 8 9 10 |
| Resists Regulations | 1 2 3 4 5 6 7 8 9 10 |
| Cruel, Sarcastic | 1 2 3 4 5 6 7 8 9 10 |
| Doesn't Give Recognition | 1 2 3 4 5 6 7 8 9 10 |
| Self-sufficient | 1 2 3 4 5 6 7 8 9 10 |
| Domineering | 1 2 3 4 5 6 7 8 9 10 |
| Opinionated | 1 2 3 4 5 6 7 8 9 10 |
| Proud | 1 2 3 4 5 6 7 8 9 10 |
| Cunning | 1 2 3 4 5 6 7 8 9 10 |

### B Score _____
#### 200

| | |
|---|---|
| Natural Talent | 1 2 3 4 5 6 7 8 9 10 |
| Analytical | 1 2 3 4 5 6 7 8 9 10 |
| Perfectionist | 1 2 3 4 5 6 7 8 9 10 |
| Conscientious | 1 2 3 4 5 6 7 8 9 10 |
| Loyal | 1 2 3 4 5 6 7 8 9 10 |
| Aesthetic | 1 2 3 4 5 6 7 8 9 10 |
| Idealistic | 1 2 3 4 5 6 7 8 9 10 |
| Sensitive | 1 2 3 4 5 6 7 8 9 10 |
| Self-sacrificing | 1 2 3 4 5 6 7 8 9 10 |
| Self-disciplined | 1 2 3 4 5 6 7 8 9 10 |
| Moody | 1 2 3 4 5 6 7 8 9 10 |
| Negative | 1 2 3 4 5 6 7 8 9 10 |
| Critical | 1 2 3 4 5 6 7 8 9 10 |
| Resists Change | 1 2 3 4 5 6 7 8 9 10 |
| Self-conscious | 1 2 3 4 5 6 7 8 9 10 |
| Unpredictable | 1 2 3 4 5 6 7 8 9 10 |
| Revengeful | 1 2 3 4 5 6 7 8 9 10 |
| Lacks Self-confidence | 1 2 3 4 5 6 7 8 9 10 |
| Unsociable | 1 2 3 4 5 6 7 8 9 10 |
| Theoretical | 1 2 3 4 5 6 7 8 9 10 |

### D Score _____
#### 200

| | |
|---|---|
| Calm, Quiet | 1 2 3 4 5 6 7 8 9 10 |
| Easy Going | 1 2 3 4 5 6 7 8 9 10 |
| Likeable | 1 2 3 4 5 6 7 8 9 10 |
| Diplomatic | 1 2 3 4 5 6 7 8 9 10 |
| Efficient, Organised | 1 2 3 4 5 6 7 8 9 10 |
| Dependable, Stable | 1 2 3 4 5 6 7 8 9 10 |
| Conservative | 1 2 3 4 5 6 7 8 9 10 |
| Practical | 1 2 3 4 5 6 7 8 9 10 |
| Reluctant Leader | 1 2 3 4 5 6 7 8 9 10 |
| Dry Humour | 1 2 3 4 5 6 7 8 9 10 |
| Unmotivated | 1 2 3 4 5 6 7 8 9 10 |
| Unexcitable | 1 2 3 4 5 6 7 8 9 10 |
| Avoids Conflict | 1 2 3 4 5 6 7 8 9 10 |
| Spectator | 1 2 3 4 5 6 7 8 9 10 |
| Selfish | 1 2 3 4 5 6 7 8 9 10 |
| Stingy | 1 2 3 4 5 6 7 8 9 10 |
| Stubborn | 1 2 3 4 5 6 7 8 9 10 |
| Self-protective | 1 2 3 4 5 6 7 8 9 10 |
| Indecisive | 1 2 3 4 5 6 7 8 9 10 |
| Fear of Risk | 1 2 3 4 5 6 7 8 9 10 |

*Instructions*
Review your management temperament test. Record each temperament trait receiving a score of seven or more. Place an 'X' in the score column corresponding with the score of each trait being listed.

Your management temperament profile consists of all of your management temperament traits receiving a score of seven or more regardless of their management temperament classification.

*Dominators*
Management Temperament Dominators are those traits receiving a score of 7–8. These management temperament traits tend to dominate the other 'weaker' traits.

*Regulators*
Management Temperament Regulators are those traits receiving a score of 9–10. They represent the strongest drive in one's management temperament makeup and provide the greatest input toward how the manager acts or reacts in a given management situation.

| MANAGEMENT TEMPERAMENT TRAIT | 7 | 8 | 9 | 10 |
|---|---|---|---|---|
| | | | | |
| | | | | |
| | | | | |
| | | | | |
| | | | | |
| | | | | |

### Scoring Instructions
1. Each temperament trait has a value from one to ten (one being the least and ten being the greatest). Circle the number you feel best indicates your level of strength or weakness in each trait.
2. After completing the test, add the total score in each temperament category (A, B, C, D) and place it on the total score line for that category in the scoring table below.
3. Your highest score represents your dominant management temperament and your second highest score represents your subdominant.

| | SCORING TABLE | | |
|---|---|---|---|
| | Total Score | | |
| A  PROMOTIONAL MANAGER | _____ 200 | = | _____ % |
| B  CONCEPT MANAGER | _____ 200 | = | _____ % |
| C  OPERATIONAL MANAGER | _____ 200 | = | _____ % |
| D  NEGOTIATING MANAGER | _____ 200 | = | _____ % |

*Figure 8. Management Temperaments*[4]

* * *

'*The DiSC Dimensions of Behavior*' is another very popular leadership tool. Again there are four categories which also in some ways parallel the four basic temperaments.

D – Dominance. (Choleric)
Motivated to solve problems and get immediate results. Tends to question the status quo. Prefers direct answers, varied activities and independence. 'I like being my own boss.' 'I know what I want and I go after it.' 'I like to test myself with new challenges.'

i – Influence. (Sanguine)
Motivated to persuade and influence others. Tends to be open and verbalises thoughts and feelings. Prefers working with people rather than alone. 'I enjoy telling stories and entertaining people.' 'I get fired up about things.' 'I like freedom from control and detail.'

S – Steadiness. (Melancholic)
Motivated to create a stable, organised environment. Tends to be patient and a good listener. Prefers participating in a group rather than directing it and listening more than talking. 'I like working with people who get along.' 'I enjoy helping people.' 'I can be counted on to get the job done.'

C – Conscientiousness. (Phlegmatic)
Motivated to achieve high personal standards. Tends to be diplomatic and carefully weighs pros and cons. Prefers environments with clearly defined expectations. 'I enjoy analysing things.' 'I am uncomfortable with emotional situations.' 'I enjoy working with people who are organised and have high standards.'

There are 'personal profile' questionaires which a person can complete and score and their behavioural tendencies and their preferences can then be mapped out.

to administer. An important aspect is also to encourage team members not only to score themselves, but also to score each other. This 'criss-cross' use can help the transparency and teachability of the team unit. These comparisons not only help in the initial disclosure phase of team formation, but also in the ongoing team building process. In this way the tests allow team members to recognise and acknowledge the strengths and weaknesses in each other.

I often stress that none of these tests pigeon-hole a person into an immutable box for life. God, and so the team, accepts them as they are, but loves them too much to leave them as he finds them! Correctly understood, the tests enable a person to continue to shine at their strengths, but also to resolve their weaknesses. It would therefore be advantageous for a team to repeat the test on an annual basis. In this way a team can ensure that all members of the team continue to play to their strengths and work on their weaknesses.

## Window of the soul

The Indians have a saying, 'Never judge a man till you have walked a mile in his moccasins.' Often the process of team building and identifying with the other members of the team can be threaded with all kinds of assumptions, misunderstandings and miscommunication. A standard tool to help in this process is the 'Johari Window'. The 'Johari Window' was developed by psychologists John Luft and Harry Ingram. They picture a window with four panes through which people see different aspects of each other's lives. When taken together a true picture of a person emerges:

| | | | |
|---|---|---|---|
| Pane 1. | Public pane | Known to self | Known to others |
| Pane 2. | Blind pane | Unknown to self | Known to others |
| Pane 3. | Private pane | Known to self | Unknown to others |
| Pane 4. | Unknown pane | Unknown to self | Unknown to others |

The four 'Panes' are never of equal size but as transparency, vulnerability and openness increase among team members, the 'panes' will change in proportion to one another. The ideal relationships

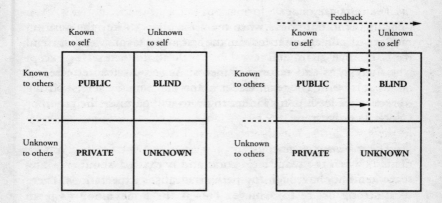

*Figure 9. The Johari Window[5]*

are when the 'public pane' is large and the other 'panes' are small. This reflects when we are most open and transparent and most enlightened in our relationships. The willingness to receive constructive feedback from others is probably the key factor which unlocks the window into our soul. As a team it is important for each team member to slowly enlarge the 'public pane' by steadily decreasing both the 'blind pane' and the 'private pane'. The 'unknown pane' will, over time, also decrease as a person discovers, through relating with others, more about themselves and so unlocks their full potential and possibilities.

## Marrying the members

It takes time to build trust and rapport in any relationship. In the adjustment to marriage, every couple will experience these three stages: 'enchantment', 'disenchantment' and then 'maturity' (see also pp. 55–8). Likewise teams, although focused on the completion of a task, need also to build secure relationships and so will also go through stages. Charles Olson, in *Cultivating Religious Growth Groups*, has identified four developmental stages in the team formation process.[6]

### 1. *The discovery stage*
This is the initial phase when team members jockey for position and try to gain acceptance from the rest of the team. Members tend to be on their guard and reveal very little about themselves, except their strengths and accomplishments! As self-disclosure increases so trust is built. The team leader in this stage must exercise strong directive leadership, for failure to do so will paralyse the group or block its growth.

### 2. *The romance stage*
This is when the team feels good and is excited about working together. They have high and perhaps idealistic expectations. There is a strong desire to achieve. This is the honeymoon as team members are often on their best behaviour with each other. It can be the lull before the storm.

### 3. *The struggle stage*
This stage is the most critical for a team. The initial glamour and idealism of being on the team begins to fade. It is characterised by confusion, conflict, pessimism, and uncertainty about the future. There is a strong desire to quit. Some sources of struggle are:

1. Rivalry over certain positions, including the leadership.
2. Discovery of irritating mannerisms and habits.
3. Refusal to face up to blockages to team unity.
4. Feelings of being excluded.
5. Disillusionment over unfulfilled expectations.
6. Uncertainty over future ministry role on the team.
7. Dominating team member.
8. Challenges to change in personal or ministerial areas.

This is the 'B zone' or danger zone. I can identify with some of these steps. At times in my own experience I have entertained such questions as: 'Do I really want to be on this team?' 'Do I ever want to be on any team again?' 'Is this what it means to be on a team?' 'Can I ever feel comfortable with her/him?' 'Can I ever have a successful relationship with them?' 'Will we ever get beyond this struggle to productivity?' You may also begin to say to yourself: 'I did not join up for this!' 'I did not leave my previous position/job/team/country for this!' 'I was better off where I was before!' 'These people have no idea what it means to be on a team!' 'It has not worked out, it is time for me to quit and move on!'

A team can move in one of three directions during this inevitable struggle:

1. It can disband, deciding the struggle is too intense and not worth the effort.
2. It can superficially address the problems and carry on with unresolved issues.
3. It can persevere through the struggle to become a healthy, honest and productive ministry unit.

The first two choices will result in unresolved conflict, unhealed hurts, self-doubts and an overcautious approach to future ministry. The third option, although at times not always the easiest or even the most attractive, is the pathway to a deep appreciation and understanding of others.

### 4. *The investment stage*
This is when the team begins to appreciate that the pain of the struggle was worthwhile and begins to work through some of the issues. Whereas the members once entertained thoughts of leaving, they now gladly make long-term commitments. This stage is characterised by personal satisfaction, a sense of achievement, realism, a healthy perspective on the team and personal ministry, optimism, expectation for the future. Skills are developed to handle future struggles and tensions.

### Forming, storming and performing

These stages have been summarised as: forming, storming and performing. Over a period of time, any of these stages may reappear, particularly when a new team member joins or when circumstances demand fresh objectives and new ways of operating. There is always the constant challenge for the individual as well as the team to keep working at being a team. No ministry or team ever arrives or stands still. 'Success is a journey, not a destination.' So likewise we can affirm that 'Teamwork is a journey not a destination.' Henry Ford defined teamwork well when he said:

> Coming together is a beginning;
> Keeping together is progress;
> Working together is success.[7]

## Know your place

Rugby provides a host of different examples of team ministry. Putting great individual players together does not necessarily always make for a great team. International players who hardly know each other need to learn not just to play with each other, but also to play for each other. Training sessions before the Five Nations games start is when players have the opportunity to be together. The coaches need to build a collection of individuals into a team. The players learn to play to each other's strengths. Each member of the squad is given an assignment on the field and through the process of training and playing together discovers what they can do well and what others can do better. In rugby, the fifteen-man team combines many skills; no one person is skilful enough to play in all positions. Admittedly there are the generalists, the utility players, but most players have a specific role to play – perhaps in the forwards or the backs, as a kicker, tackler, jumper, throw-in, runner, etc. The strongest team is the team in which each player knows his position/assignment and plays it well. What team training is to rugby, team building is to team ministry.

Which players should be included in the team? What positions should be filled for a balanced team ministry? In rugby the positions are predetermined by the rules of the game. How should they be determined in team ministry? Management and team consultants today recognise that although the formal role of each team member is important, the informal role played by each member is just as vital for the balance and health of a team. Most teams focus on selecting a person solely for the position they will fill, rather than seeing the whole personality contribution they will bring to a team.

## Personality roles

Meredith Belbin has studied team function for twenty-eight years at Cambridge and has run countless 'Teamopoly' seminars for managerial teams. His book, *Management Teams: Why They Succeed or Fail*, coupled with his management video, *Building a Perfect Team*, have become current management landmarks. Belbin observes that although team members may have their specific titles and formal job descriptions, they also fulfil 'personality team roles'. He maintains that a team given the right balance of personality roles, as well as job roles, will have a dynamic that will keep it both creative and successful.

In constructing a team, it is vital to blend not only the job roles but also the personality roles. Most teams are built only around job roles and often with people who share a very narrow personality band. Contributions from both roles is necessary. Effective teams, however, tend to have both a wide diversity of roles and personality, rather than people who are similar in temperament and outlook; whereas ineffective teams tend to be unbalanced, having too many people who are too alike.

Divergence of personality may admittedly make the initial 'struggle stage' more difficult, but in the long run it will undoubtedly increase the team's dynamic, creativity and effectiveness. My observation of teams would confirm the fact that every team member's contribution to the team is more than just fulfilling their job descriptions. Most informal roles are usually filled by the team members naturally, spontaneously, even unconsciously and help the team's overall productivity.

## Be on the same page

The goal in American football is to put the ball in your opponent's end zone. In essence this a simple and clear objective and superficially should make it a relatively simple game. The game is complicated, however, by a plethora of rules and regulations as to what a team can and cannot do during the course of the exercise. Matters are complicated still further by the wide range of various strategies used by both the offensive and defensive playing units of both teams. Players have to learn and memorise their team's bible, the playbook. Each play is coded by numbers and letters. It is crucial for each player to know each page of play perfectly. Sometimes the play on the field looks rather chaotic with players going in all directions! In actuality it is very regimented. Every player is allocated a particular assignment; either running, tackling, blocking or passing, so as to confuse and confound the opposition and so get the ball down-field. It is vital each team player knows his specific role and does it effectively so that the team as a whole is successful. In the heat of the game they all need to be on the same page. The team huddle is usually the moment when the quarterback, the team captain, calls the specific strategy or play they will be using. The players then leave the huddle pumped up to take up their respective positions on the line and hopefully make a successful move against the opposition.

There are more problems in team ministry caused by role dilemma than almost anything else. It can in fact spawn a whole cache of problems. On the one hand, some members seem reluctant to follow their agreed defined role on the team. They do not readily accept that they are not to play the central role of the quarterback, or to receive the acclaim of scoring and spiking the ball as a wide receiver. Their role and call is different but just as vital as the unsung linebacker in the trenches. This aspect of role dilemma is usually born out of a misguided ambition.

The other side of role dilemma is when the member's role or assignment has not been clearly spelled out. They are genuinely confused and frustrated as to what is expected of them. This frustration is born out of lack of organisation and preparation of the team, particularly by the leader. Unless these frustrations are resolved, then serious conflict can emerge in the team and threaten its effectiveness and fruitfulness. We will be exploring the results of role dilemma in more detail in a later chapter.

In American football after most downs, the offensive players gather together in their huddle, and the quarterback indicates which play they will be seeking to execute. The players then go to their positions and carry out their respective assignments. Each player has grasped the fact that their role is a vital contribution to the total team effort and success. If they 'blow' their assignment then the whole play could be disrupted and the team make no progress down the field.

During one of our pastoral team meetings we were discussing this picture of teamwork. We recognised that each of the team comes together in the huddle (pastoral team meeting); we hear the play (we renew our sense of mission and vision); we take up our team assignment (we organise our respective areas of responsibility: youth, children, music, visitation, preaching, etc); we move the ball down field (we impact our community for Christ). In other words, 'We gather to scatter.'

This football parallel is undoubtedly an excellent way of illustrating certain aspects of team ministry. It illustrates the importance of a common vision and clear objectives. It underlines the diversity of abilities and gifts that are needed to get the job done. It illustrates the need for decisive leadership. It emphasises the specific responsibilities/assignments each team member must have, and must be clear about. It shows how team members must subordinate their own preferences/plans for the common good. It makes the point that in a team there is a synergistic result to our efforts; we do achieve more together than we ever could do apart.

As I reflected on this I came to realise that the illustration, if pushed too far, produces an individualism which is unhelpful to the true concept of team ministry. The idea of a huddle could imply that we come together and then we do our own thing. We receive our marching orders and then we each move away to do our own individual task or ministry. A team could then end up pulling in different directions. For a team to remain committed to a true team ministry, the arrows need to be reversed – they need to moving towards the vision, not away from it. In this way the whole team stays focused in on its mission and vision.

The picture is a constant reminder of the need to share resources

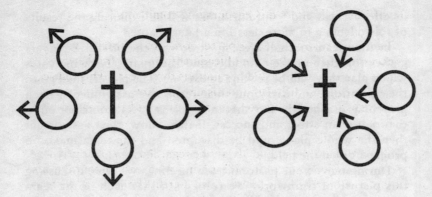

*Figure 10. The Team Huddle*

and responsibilities. Every team member is not somewhere out in left field running their own route. It is a centralised rather than a decentralised approach to team ministry. This guards against a protectionism that can creep into teams. People guard their area and resist changes to: financial resources; human resources; restructuring of programs; redeploying of personnel; cancelling well-worn tired programs; altering tried-and-trusted approaches to ministry. In other words, they become reluctant to change or adapt to a changing ministry environment. This can, at worst, lead to kingdom building – instead of building the kingdom. At best it will lead to maintaining a white elephant—instead of running with the hounds. The illustration of a centralised ministry approach is a constant reminder that we will all do whatever it takes to get the job done. It is not my ministry, per se, that becomes my goal, but it is the total team ministry and vision which becomes the overarching goal.

The apostle Paul asked, 'Who is sufficient for these things?' (2 Cor. 2:16). 'Who is equal to the task?' Who indeed? At times it can seem like an overwhelming task! The motivational management message reminds us that:

No one gets ahead.
No one gets behind.
And all are rewarded.
This is teamwork.[8]

David Cormack offers this encouraging comment:

> The time taken for groups to come to maturity varies according to size, the style of leadership and the frequency of meetings etc. A good rule of thumb is three years! This figure always calls up disbelief and dismay in teams, yet it is better to realistic about how long it takes than to be dismayed by lack of progress.[9]

Being part of a team should always be regarded as a great privilege. We have co-workers alongside of us, who can encourage and exhort us along the way. But it is also a great challenge as we learn to work with others. Team must become 'S.T.E.A.M.' with the Spirit of God helping us to become all he has planned and purposed for us, both individually as team members and collectively as a team.

# 7

# Team play

Over recent years I have had to work through a couple of very difficult conflict situations with other pastors on our pastoral teams. It would be inappropriate for me to go into all the details but suffice it to say that they were extremely difficult and painful times. In both instances the pastors concerned were different to me in personality and style of ministry and so we complemented each other well. Superficially, as a team we were a good fit, with different strengths and weaknesses. The pastors concerned had many fine qualities which I appreciated and respected.

## The honeymoon is over

It soon became apparent, however, not just to me but also to others in leadership, that in both cases the pastors were somewhat insecure. They would stress the need for relationships, but would not give the necessary time to build them, either with me or anyone else. They would skip agreed meetings, arrive late or leave early. Despite plenty of positive affirmation and encouragement, they both had a tendency to resist any kind of criticism, feedback or evaluation from anyone, particularly if it could be taken negatively. If they were challenged directly on an issue, or if they did not get their own way, they would sometimes withdraw emotionally and occasionally sulk for days. They would thus manipulate the situation to avoid dealing with the issue. Their usual response when challenged would be, 'What's your problem?

Why don't you trust me? Until we have a deeper relationship you have not earned the right to criticise me!' Their avoidance behaviour made it difficult to build a deep relationship with either of them. It seemed that we were going round in circles and getting nowhere fast!

My initial response, in both cases, was a reluctance to force the issue and confront the problems that we obviously had in our relationship. This was due to a number of factors: my inexperience; my sense of shame, even embarrassment, that the relationship was not going well, despite public appearances; and a fear of the consequences of an all-out confrontation. Looking back, I now realise, in my protectiveness, I made a serious error of judgment. I hung back from pressing the issue into a full confrontation which I feared could become public, damaging the church, their ministry and perhaps even me. I now know I should have risked the consequences and taken the initiative much earlier. Eventually, in both instances, I did face up to facts and seek to resolve the underlying issues which then began the long process of confrontation and conflict resolution.

With hindsight, I know that I could have been a better team leader; that I should have said and done things differently; that it was not all their fault. The key issue, however, in both situations was the reluctance these associates had in accepting their role as an associate pastor/team member and mine as the senior pastor/team leader. They both had had a history of struggling with spiritual authority. In one instance it took nine months, with two deacons acting as mediators, to resolve the issue and see our personal relationship improve and deepen as we drew closer together. In the other instance the pastor moved on, the key heart issue sadly being left unresolved.

Perhaps these were just extremely unfortunate, even unusually difficult team experiences? I wish that were so! The details may be different, but as I have talked with team leaders and team members from a wide variety of situations, I have sadly discovered that others have had similar experiences. No one goes into a marriage looking for a divorce, yet over 40 per cent end that way; even Christian marriages are not immune. The same is true of team ministry. Team members go in with the best of intentions, but it does not always work out. How many teams experience real difficulty? Impossible to say definitively, but from my contacts with others I would say many do, although very few are prepared to admit it!

The general lesson that I have learnt is that when there is tension and conflict in a team, it will not go away. It needs to be recognised, challenged, confronted and resolved, one way or the other. The specific lesson I have learned from my experiences is that every team needs a clearly recognised leader. If that position is questioned or challenged by a member of the team, then it should be dealt with decisively.

## Defining conflict

*Chamber's Dictionary* defines conflict as:

> A trial of strength between opposed parties or principles. A violent collision, a struggle or contest, a battle, a mental struggle, to fight, contend, to be in opposition, to clash, to be at odds with, contradictory. From the Latin, con, together, and fligere, to strike.[1]

Conflict occurs when there is a perceived divergence of interests or goals – a situation in which two or more human beings desire goals which they perceive as being attainable by one or the other but not by both. It is the belief that both parties' goals cannot be achieved simultaneously. Conflict has been described as two cars trying to occupy the same space at the same time or two lions claiming the same territory.

Whenever people get close together, whether in marriage or ministry, then conflict is inevitable. In itself, conflict is: neutral (neither good nor bad); natural (not to be avoided nor denied); normal (neither your particular problem nor necessarily your fault); and indeed healthy (part of being a human being and a leader). Conflict should be viewed as being common to all human relationships as people interact closely with each other. The goal of a team should not be to ensure the absence of conflict, but to be equipped with the ability to handle and resolve conflict in an honest and healthy way. It is unresolved conflict, not conflict as such, that can damage relationships.

As Norman Shawchuck correctly observes:

> If Jesus could not live in this world without conflict, we might as well accept it; we too will have conflict in our churches and ministries. Conflict is a normal part of the church . . . Conflict however, is not sinful of itself. Sinfulness in conflict, results from the way we behave in the conflict, not from disagreement or tensions between us. Paul knew from experience there could be conflict without sin, and encouraged us to 'be angry and do not sin' (Ephesians 4:26).[2]

## Biblical conflict

The Bible is a refreshingly honest book. In its pages we do not find plastic saints with their faults and failings painted over. Instead we discover people made of flesh and blood, warts and all. From Genesis to Revelation there is a tendency in all human relationships, in and outside the church, toward brokenness. There will be disagreements, some of which will result in conflict. Others will not only result in conflict, but also in sin. Conflict began with Adam and Eve (Gen. 3). It spread to their sons Cain and Abel (Gen. 4). It exploded during the days of Noah (Gen. 6). It culminated in the Tower of Babel (Gen. 11).

Examples abound in the Early Church even among some of the pillars of the Church: the controversy with the Grecian widows (Acts 6); the Jerusalem Council (Acts 15); Paul and Barnabas (Acts 15); Paul and Peter (Gal. 2); Euodia and Syntyche (Phil. 4); Jesus at the Temple (Matt. 21); Jesus's specific teaching on handling conflict (Matt. 5).

Conflict has been part of our world since Adam and Eve chose to conflict with God's will. Those first parents then saw the conflict between their two sons leading one to kill the other. Conflict and killing has continued to escalate over the centuries. War is not the only tragic expression of conflict. All around us we see its mark: husbands and wives; parents and children; brothers and sisters; friends and neighbours; students and teachers; and the list goes on. We live in a world filled with the tragic consequences of conflict.

As Paul Cedar sadly observes:

> Perhaps the greatest tragedy though, is the conflict taking place in our churches and in the relationships of professing Christians. Almost daily I receive word of a church being divided by conflict or a pastor being separated from his spouse or a Christian ministry being under attack by another.[3]

My experience in teams has been overwhelmingly positive and delightful. But I have also had my share of negative experiences. As a member of four pastoral teams over a period of twenty years, conflict was present in some form or another in each team. It may not have been recognised, acknowledged or dealt with by all concerned but it was nevertheless present. Over the years I have learnt not how to hide it, but how to handle it. As I have talked with team leaders, from a wide variety of Christian churches and organisations, I have yet to find a team in which conflict of one kind or another has not been an issue at some time. Over the years, I have discovered ways in which team leaders and team members can be helped to recognise and to resolve conflict in a healthy manner.

### Being pulled apart

Not all conflicts are the same: there are different types of conflict. Conflicts can be grouped according to first, who the conflict is between; and second, what the conflict is about. In the former case, most people assign conflicts to one of four categories.

1.  Intra-personal: conflict within an individual, personal struggles.
2.  Inter-personal: conflict between individuals.
3.  Intra-group: conflict within members of a group or team.
4.  Inter-group: conflict between different groups or organisations.

The different categories do not mean that each can be neatly compartmentalised away from each other. One type of conflict can lead to another, particularly if it is left unresolved.

In the second grouping, conflicts are categorised as:

1. Substantive: conflicts over facts, means, ends and values.
2. Attitudinal: conflicts over feelings, perspectives and prejudices.

## 1. Intra-personal conflicts

These are the struggles which a person has within themselves. Inner conflict involves the unresolved issues which wage war within a person. The Christian psychologist, Lawrence Crabb, based on the work of Dr Miriam Wagner, maintains that there are three basic psychological needs within a person.[4] These are the needs for: security, self-worth and significance. As a person develops and grows physically through childhood and young adulthood, they seek to meet and fulfil these basic needs. If they are not satisfied, then they become needs which drive a person and cause intra-personal conflicts.

### A. Need for security; search for affection; problem of insecurity

Every person asks the question 'What am I?' If a person lacks security then they will develop an insecure personality. This can manifest itself in a number of ways as they constantly look for approval, acceptance, assurance and affection. They have a deep need to be loved and to belong. They need and seek constant encouragement and find criticism, even the slightest negative comment, hard to handle. They do not respond well to the process of feedback, evaluation or accountability. They have a tendency to become extremely relationship-oriented at the expense of completing the task. They are quick to take the credit for any success, but distance themselves from any failures or set-backs for they have a deep fear of being rejected.

In their need to be popular and fit in with the crowd, they often play to the gallery. They tend to back off from confronting or challenging situations for which they are responsible. They can sometimes develop poor or frequent relationships in order to compensate. They often find it hard to settle down and have a tendency to roam or move on.

## B. Need for self-worth; search for acceptance; problem of inferiority

Every person also asks the question, 'Who am I?' If a person lacks positive self-worth they develop a personality characterised by inferiority. A negative self-worth can be produced by physical, social, intellectual and material deficiencies. A person may become a striver, a competitor, constantly seeking to prove themselves against others. They become the 'achievers', the 'A type' personalities who compete with themselves and everyone else. This person may often have a chip on their shoulder and is out to show themselves and the world that they are as good, if not better, than those who are more naturally endowed.

The small-man syndrome or the person born-on-the-wrong-side-of-the-tracks are classic examples of this. Shorter or poorer than everyone else, he sets out to prove that he is the best. In doing so he may walk over or step on anyone else to make it to the top. Many top sports people and entertainers are driven people, striving constantly to prove themselves. These people find it hard to believe that a person can be accepted simply for who they are, not what they can do or achieve. Success is all-important, and failure is seen as an unthinkable catastrophe. A fall does not bruise these people but breaks them into pieces. These people usually become workaholics (as they prove themselves) and/or materialists (as they provide evidence of their achievements).

Unmet needs in this area can also cause a person to be rebellious (as they hit back against an unjust world); attention seekers (as they even do wrong to be noticed); drop-outs (as they go into a corner and hide); or under-achievers (as they see the mountain is too hard to climb).

## C. Need for significance; search for approval; problem of inadequacy

Every person also asks the question, 'Why am I?' If a person does not have a sense of significance to their life they will manifest feelings of inadequacy. If a person feels that they do not have a purpose to life or are not making a useful contribution to life, they will be overwhelmed with feelings of uselessness and hopelessness. Because they lack fulfilment they are driven by frustration. Being unemployed is a devastating experience; as are being passed over in a promotion; being taken for granted; or feeling your contribution is not noticed or appreciated. All these tough experiences of life contribute towards reinforcing feelings of inadequacy.

This can drive a person to be self-centred and self-absorbed; overly critical of the contribution of others; frustrated with themselves and others; taking out their frustrations on others through verbal or physical abuse. They can displace their anger over their inadequacy on to others, which can make for difficulties in close relationships. They can overcompensate by putting on an appearance through possessions and lifestyle. Or they may seek solace through various addictions to conceal their inadequacies, such as in materialism, drugs, alcohol, etc.

## Standing on a three-legged stool

Each of these three areas can be represented by the leg of a three-legged stool. A stable personality is one in which all three legs are straight and strong. However, if one leg is seriously deficient, then the whole personality will shake and be out of balance as it rests on an uneven base. No one is perfect; we all have our inner struggles and conflicts, we are all people in process. Deep unresolved issues will mean that our personality is shaky and will be easily rocked by others close to us. Inner conflicts, therefore, do not just affect ourselves, our own peace of mind, but inevitably they spill over into our relationships with others, particularly when we draw close to others, as in marriage or in team ministry.

If there is conflict between people, the first area to explore is not the inter-personal situation alone. Begin by exploring the possibility of intra-personal struggles. More often than not, the two are linked. The psychological tests discussed in an earlier chapter could be useful resources for exploring possible intra-personal conflicts. In some ways we all need help with our past, for we all limp on through life! For some, however, the past can cripple their progress, particularly in relating closely with others. This may become apparent and so counselling may be of help to them and the team. An understanding of this whole area of intra-personal conflict can be demonstrated by the way the following statements are interpreted:

It's not what I think I am that matters.
It's not what you think I am that matters.
It's what I think you think I am that matters!

## 2. Inter-personal conflicts

This term is used to describe conflicts between two or more people. It could be conflict between: a husband and wife; a parent and child; a pastor and deacon; a pastor and staff person; team leader and team member; team member and team member; missionaries within a mission compound; Christian workers; and so on. This is probably the most common type of conflict to affect those in teams and the pastoral ministry. There are many possible causes for conflict between individuals, and we will explore these under the headings of substantive and attitudinal issues. Although acknowledging that other types of conflicts do happen, we will devote most of our ensuing study in the following chapters to recognising and resolving inter-personal types of conflicts.

## 3. Intra-group conflicts

These describe collective conflicts between members of a group with other members of the same group. The group could be a family, a pastoral team, a church leadership team, a church or an organisation. For example, within a family: parents and children; within church leadership: deacons' board and pastoral team; within a church: church members and elders. This type of conflict arises when different parties within the group feel that another group is not functioning along agreed guidelines; is not performing to expectation; or is not attaining perceived aims. Wrong perceptions, false expectations and poor communication often lie at the root of many of these conflicts. Even if these are not the initial cause, they can become causal factors in the ongoing conflict.

## 4. Inter-group conflicts

This describes the situation in which one organisation or group is at conflict with another organisation or group. For example, church against church; a church with its community; a missionary organisation at odds with another missionary organisation; within the same church: the youth group in conflict with the seniors' group; the missionary team with the evangelism team; deacons' board and the pastoral team. Many of the principles that apply to resolving inter-personal conflicts can also be applied to bringing a resolution to this type of conflict.

### Getting to the root of the problem

All four categories of conflict may be interrelated, and indeed may escalate from one to the other if they remain unresolved at any one level. The above four categories focus on who is involved in the conflict. We also need to know what the conflict is about. We need to understand what the possible root causes of the conflict might be.

## 1. Substantive issues

Conflicts can be caused because of perceived differences over facts, means, methods, policies, goals, purposes, ends, values or traditions. Warren Schmidt and Robert Tannenbaum subdivide substantive issues into various categories:[5]

### A. Conflict over facts
These can be settled by ascertaining the precise facts/details of the situation which are causing the difficulty. For example, it may concern finances, numbers in attendance, hours of work, location of a property, details of a past event, what was actually said or done, details of future plans, etc. If there has been a genuine misunderstanding or miscommunication then the matter may be resolved quite quickly. It is not unusual, however, to discover other causes, both substantive and attitudinal, layered over the facts.

## B. Conflict over values and traditions

In every group or organisation there is a common body of values, beliefs, cherished principles, traditions, etc. These are deeply held and determine the choices the group makes and the way in which it orders its life. These values shape what the person or group wants to be. They are what they want to give themselves to, in the ultimate sense. These are the principles as opposed to the preferences that people feel very deeply about and will fight tooth and nail over. In Christian circles, doctrinal and theological beliefs can become arenas of conflict and causes of dissension and division. In a team ministry it is important to distinguish between the major values (which we die for!) and the minor values (which we live with!). Sadly, many people major on minors instead of 'Keeping the main thing the main thing!'

## C. Conflict over methods and means

These include the rules the team or group is living by and the actions taken to accomplish their goals. Conflict can arise when the way in which a group or team should achieve its goal is being questioned. What is deemed permissible and acceptable to all can often cause much debate and disagreement from some members. The people involved need to distinguish carefully between: the principles at stake (the moral right ways), which are non-negotiable; and their own preferences (their own ways), which are open to being challenged and should not necessarily carry the day.

## D. Conflict over ends and goals

The stated and agreed aims of the group are obviously crucial to its very existence. 'What is the purpose of the team?' 'Why is the team or group in existence?' These are vital questions on which there must be whole-hearted agreement. The team, group or organisation exists to achieve these goals. People are working together to fulfil them. It is important, however, for the people involved to distinguish between the team or group's overarching long-term goals and the undergirding short-term goals. They are quite different. People should therefore adjust their responses accordingly.

## 2. Attitudinal issues

These are issues which cause conflict because of preconceived feelings, perspectives or prejudices. This type of conflict is one in which a person clashes against another primarily because they perceive themselves to be incompatible with the other person. False assumptions are made about others so that another person and their competence is prejudged. The conflict may be because of an attitude toward others because of their race, age, sexual gender, physical appearance, nationality, doctrinal stances, etc. These acquired prejudices, and the resultant stereotyping of others, have been formed because of upbringing, culture, education and experiences of the past. These attitudes, which the person now carries, affect the way they habitually relate to and react with those in the present. These echoes from the past cause them to make false assumptions about others and so to reverberate when placed in a close working relationship. When divergent attitudes are present, people find themselves bumping into each other in conflictual ways.

Coupled with these attitudinal issues it is not unusual to find a great deal of emotion. Larry McSwain and William Treadwell rightly observe: 'Such a prejudice has become emotionally rigid, so that logical arguments will have little effect in changing it. Efforts to change the attitude are viewed as personal attacks.'[6]

An inevitable by-product of this kind of emotional heat is the breakdown of healthy and open communication, which only exacerbates the problem. It is, therefore, vital to get those involved to face up to the real root of the problem and work through the process of unearthing it. It needs to be faced and owned, and recognised that it is not a substantive issue, but one which is an attitudinal framework of thinking.

Norman Shawchuck uses a flow diagram, based on the work of Jerry Robinson and Roy Clifford,[7] to link the different stages of conflict. He adds the extra dimension that conflict can be seen as the invasion of a person's territory. People are territorial beings who will defend their territory against attack and invasion. They do this by either going on the defensive or the offensive. If a person feels someone has trespassed on their turf then conflict will ensue. Shawchuck maintains that there are the specific 'territories of conflict' which can be invaded, and there are certain ways in which

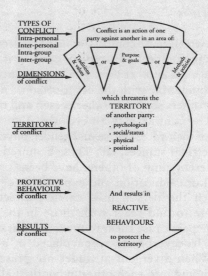

*Figure 11. Operational Model of Conflict*[8]

people defend themselves and their territory.

When you are in the midst of conflict, you need first to recognise that you are not alone. The type of conflict you may be experiencing is not unusual among Christians, even between Christian leaders. Conflict is normal, neutral, natural and healthy. Second, isolate the real issues behind what is going on, to go beyond the surface and down to the root causes.

## Cutting the grass

It is possible to spend your life cutting grass, for it just keeps on growing. If you have weeds in your lawn they too will keep on growing. As you cut them down with the grass, you can fool yourself into believing that you have dealt with them. But they will reappear and you will have to cut them down again, unless you are prepared to do something about them. It takes time, effort and energy to dig them up 'root and all' and prevent them from springing up again!

Conflicts appear on the surface of our lives but the roots lie deeper. The surface issues are only the fruit of unseen struggles, attitudes, motives and beliefs. I picture it in this way – in conflict we are faced with a situation or a difficulty which demands our attention (presenting problem). This has an immediate cause behind it (surface cause). We can usually discover this quite quickly from the surrounding circumstances. Sometimes we may need to acknowledge the fact that behind this lies a deeper unresolved issue (root problem). This can be caused by a fundamental defect in a person (foundational cause). In recognising and resolving conflict we may need to dig a bit deeper. This is not to dig up the dirt on a person. In order to prevent us forever simply cutting the grass we need to get to 'root' of the problem. We need to deal thoroughly with the situation so that it will not be a recurring problem for all concerned. Time, energy and effort are needed to resolve success-fully all the underlying issues and prevent further weeds from growing. As the writer to the Hebrews reminds us: 'See to it that no-one misses the grace of God and that no bitter root grows up to cause trouble and defile many' (Heb. 12:15).

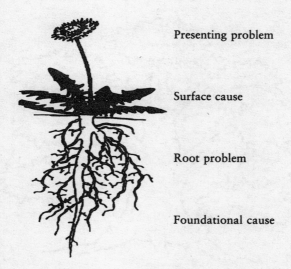

Presenting problem

Surface cause

Root problem

Foundational cause

*Figure 12. The Root of the Problem*

## Roots, shoots and offshoots

David Cormack, in *Peacing Together: From Conflict to Resolution*, provides some excellent insights into resolving conflict. He observes that conflict often arises through mishandled relationships, or mishandled leadership. This results in selfish desires taking over and taking root in the situation. If the axe is not laid to the root and the problem/conflict not dealt with quickly, then several branches and foliage will begin to grow from the unresolved conflict.

He suggests that at the root of all continuing unresolved conflict is selfishness. Perhaps, a better word might be self-seeking or a carnal rather than a God-glorifying spiritual resolution to the relationship. The way we relate to and react with one another in close personal and working relationships is often less than perfect. A person may be offensive in their approach, which may then spark off a defensive or offensive response and so the seed has been planted. This selfishness, or carnality, in turn causes branches of fear, shame, guilt, blame, denial, and avoidance. These in turn cause clumps of foliage: anxiety and phobias, loss of self-esteem,

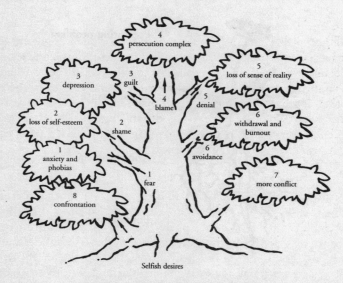

*Figure 13. The Roots, Shoots and Offshoots of Conflict*[9]

depression, persecution complex, loss of sense of reality, withdrawal and burnout, more conflict and confrontation.[10]

## Fear

When a situation of conflict begins to emerge and is then left unresolved, we can react in a number of ways as we defend our territory. In most conflicts fear is present in some form or another. It may not be acknowledged but it is present. Fear that the situation will become known to others; fear of what others may think of us, the team, the church; fear of what the person may say or do; fear that we might be wrong and lose; fear of the consequences. Excessive fear can lead to anxiety and even phobias as we battle on.

## Shame

This fear leads to shame and loss of self-esteem as we struggle with coming to terms with the situation. We feel ashamed that as Christians, or even as Christian leaders, we have been unable to resolve our differences. We feel acutely embarrassed at our thoughts, wrong attitudes and actions, the harsh words we have spoken and the ways in which we have reacted or responded in the conflict.

## Guilt and Blame

Guilt and possible depression run hard on the heels of shame as we feel a sense of worthlessness and unworthiness. In the midst of our guilt, instead of seeking a resolution to the root of the conflict, we can simply blame others, whom we view as the villains of the plot. We then lapse into feelings of paranoia. This unchecked downward spiral results in us interpreting others' actions from only one particular viewpoint and so we end up with a biased perspective and a possible persecution complex.

## Denial

The surprising thing is that when most of us are locked in combat with someone in conflict, we do all we can to deny that we are! Our denial is usually quite subtle. We may readily admit to the presence of a problem, but not to the seriousness of the situation. Unable to face up honestly to our differences, we are unable to deal effectively with them. It is often particularly hard for Christians to come to terms with conflict and to face up to it and so to deal with it. This is usually due to a belief and commitment to unity. We mistakenly believe that in admitting to conflict we will be undermining our integrity and so the ability to minister to others. Denial leads to a loss of reality, as we find it hard to come to terms with failure in a relationship, or in one aspect of our ministry. Denying a conflict's existence, however, does not cause it to go away. It will tend to be forced underground where it will eat away at the foundations of our relationship with that person, and in all probability undermine other relationships as well.

## Avoidance

For some the only solace is to withdraw. This may involve an emotional detachment from the person or situation. They are still there, but they are no longer fully present. For others the avoidance is a physical one. They deliberately avoid the person or situation by having as little contact with them as possible. This may involve missing scheduled team meetings completely or perhaps simply arriving late or leaving early. Excuses about a busy schedule or urgent appointments are made. The truth of the matter is that avoidance and detachment are occurring. The long-term effect on all concerned can be extremely wearing. Withdrawal is no answer for the deep malaise afflicting the person and, if untreated, will eventually cause emotional, spiritual and even physical exhaustion. It is hard to keep up the pretence indefinitely.

In the struggle to cope in the situation, to continue an effective ministry and contend with their seclusion, the person usually suffers burn-out. If left unresolved, this will in turn lead to more conflict and so the tree continues to blossom with devastating long-term effects for all those involved.

# 8

# Team effort

It was a hot summer's day. I was in a rush and had to drive to the bank to get some cash. My luck was in, I spotted an empty parking space right near the entrance to the bank. As I drove towards it, to my consternation someone else was also heading for the same space. We both arrived at the same time! Who had the right to claim the space? I was absolutely sure that I had seen it first! A thought crossed my mind, perhaps the person in the other car attended our church; I had better be gracious and be a good example and witness! With a weak plastic smile and a cheery wave of the hand, I went off in search of that elusive space! Two cars each trying to occupy the same space at the same time: a recipe for tension, for collision, for conflict.

It's the couple's golden wedding anniversary, the cameras are there to record the happy event. The interviewer asks the obvious hackneyed question, 'So how have you managed to remain married, to stay the course and stick together for fifty years?' 'Well, we've never had a cross word between us over the years,' the proud husband replies, and his dutiful wife nods heartily in agreement. 'That's our recipe for happiness, never a cross word.' Most other married couples watching the interview are either incredulous ('That can't be right!'), or envious ('What's wrong with us?'), for that certainly has not been true of their experience.

The possible explanation of this apparent marital bliss, is that one of the couple has assumed the role of the boss, while the other has found their place as the doormat. Admittedly, this may make for domestic peace, but it suppresses personal growth, individual maturity, promotion of individual creativity and freedom of expression. It has been said of the marriage relationship that 'If two people agree on everything, then one of them is not necessary!'

Whenever people get close together in personal or working relationships, whether in marriage or ministry, then conflict is neutral, natural, normal and indeed healthy. Conflict is common to all human relationships. Teams working closely together need not become paranoid at the presence of conflict, but need to be equipped with the necessary skills to handle and resolve conflict constructively.

> To be, or not to be: that is the question:
> Whether 'tis nobler in the mind to suffer
> The slings and arrows of outrageous fortune,
> Or to take arms against a sea of troubles,
> And by opposing end them?   (William Shakespeare, *Hamlet*)

Hamlet knew the struggle of conflict, and the temptation to avoid confronting its cause. So have many leaders. There is the temptation to sweep conflict under the carpet, to ignore it and hope it will go away. If we push this illustration to an extreme – suppose you find a pile of dust and you lift up the carpet edge and sweep it away out of sight. You can walk on the carpet without even noticing the dirt lying under it. Suppose you do the same thing every week. Weeks and months go by; the piles of dust accumulate under the carpet; they gather into large lumps, out of sight, but still present under the carpet. They produce ridges and bumps all over the carpet so that you have to consciously step over them as you walk on the carpet. Yet you continue to pretend that there is nothing wrong, you continue to sweep further piles of dust under the carpet, adding to the problem. Ridiculous, I hear you say! Yet many team leaders and team members do just that as they continue to sweep the tensions and difficulties under the carpet, hoping that somehow they will just disappear. An out of sight, out of mind approach to the problem. What they need to do is to face the challenge of cleaning up. This can be a big job, so where do you start?

## Conflict styles

The place to begin is to become aware of the way that you are most likely to react in a conflict situation. In an earlier chapter we examined the various ways in which people differentiate the different personality types. That can be a help. There are also several tools that have been devised specifically to help understand the way that people react when faced with conflict.

*Peacing together*

People are different, and so the way in which people approach conflict will differ from one person to another. David Augsburger, in *Caring Enough to Confront*, produces a very helpful diagram which he calls the 'Affirmation/Assertiveness Circle' and which 'visualizes the inter-relationship of caring and confronting, of love and power, of concern about relationships and concern for goals'. He summarises people's approach to conflict management by maintaining that there are only five options available.[1]

*1. Your way. 9/1. yield*
High concern for relationship. Little concern for goals.
I give in. You win – I lose.
I-yield-to-be-nice-since-I-need-your-friendship.

*2. No way. 1/1. Withdraw*
Little concern for relationship. Little concern for goals.
I want out. I leave – I lose.
I-am-uncomfortable-so-I-will-withdraw.

*3. My way. 1/9. Compete*
Little concern for relationship. High concern for goals.
I must win. I win – you lose.
I-am-right-you-are-wrong.

*4. No one's way. 5/5. Compromise*
Moderate concern for relationship. Moderate concern for goals.
I will meet you halfway. I lose – you lose.
I-have-only-half-the-truth-and-I-need-your-half.

*5. Our way. 9/9. Resolve*
High concern for relationship. High concern for goals.
I can care and confront. I win – you win.
I-want-relationship-and-I-also-want-honesty-and-integrity.

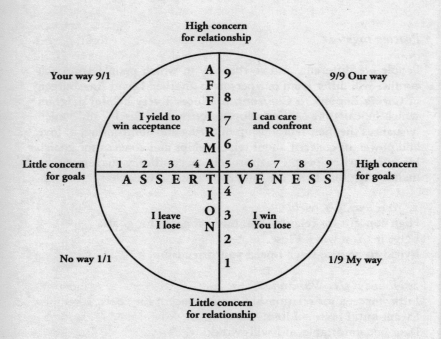

Figure 14. *Affirmation/Assertiveness Circle*[2]

*Animal instincts*

Norman Shawchuck produces a grid of the different management styles, balancing the person's concern for relationships with their concern for personal goals/interests, and he too maintains that there are five basic conflict management styles. He compares the ways in which people react to conflict to that of a particular type of animal.[3] David Johnson and Frank Johnson have captured these instinctive ways in which people respond to conflict in a helpful diagram (Figure 15).

*1. The Teddy Bear. Smoothing. Accommodating.*
High relationships and low personal goals.
Sanguine temperament.
This style seeks to preserve the relationship at all costs by initially denying and ignoring conflict. Then by appealing to 'forgive and forget'; by appeasing others through conceding ground, blaming self and accommodating other's desires. It is a person-orientated, yield/lose style.

*2. The Turtle. Withdrawing. Avoiding.*
Low relationships and low personal goals.
Melancholic temperament.
This style seeks to stay out of the conflict, to avoid being identified with either side, by being passive and even withdrawing. It requires the person to be unassertive, not pursuing their own interests, and supporting others to achieve their interests. It is a passive, abdicator, lose/leave style.

*3. The Shark. Forcing. Competing.*
High personal goals and low relationships.
Choleric temperament.
This style is intent on winning. The person assumes there are only two possible outcomes: winning or losing – and that winning is preferable to losing. Prime importance is placed on achieving their own goals at the expense of others'; willingness to sacrifice relationships in order to accomplish these goals. Often a low self-esteem pushes them to win at any cost. Assumes that persuasion, power and coercion are legitimate means to achieve ends. It is a

task-orientated, domineering, controlling, win/lose style.

*4. The Fox. Compromising. Bargaining.*
Moderate relationships and moderate goals.
Phlegmatic temperament.
This style seeks to provide each side with a little bit of winning in
order to persuade each to accept a little bit of losing, for the common
good. Assertion, flexibility, persuasion and sometimes even
manipulation are required to satisfy the needs of both sides. 'We
must all submit our personal desires to serve the larger community.'
It is a negotiation, conciliation, win a little/lose a little style.

*5. The Owl. Confronting. Collaborating.*
High relationships and high personal goals.
Blended temperament.
This style seeks to get all the parties fully involved in defining the
conflict and in carrying out mutually agreeable steps for resolving
it. Emphasis is placed on achieving the goals of all the members, co-
operative working through of differences, safeguarding the interests

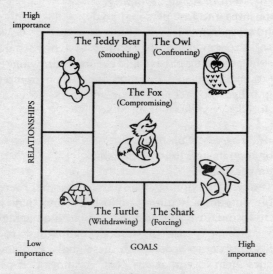

*Figure 15. Animal Instincts*[4]

of the organisation, and on maintaining the well-being of the relationships. The person is assertive, yet flexible. Their message is 'Everyone's goals are important, and if we work together we will find mutually acceptable approaches to the conflict issue.' It is an activating, total involvement, synergistic, win/win style.

## The right temperament

Which approach or style best captures the way in which you handle conflict? Let's be honest: none of us likes conflict, we all hope it will somehow just solve itself. We would all rather look the other way and pretend we did not see or hear anything. None of us wants to get involved and have to sort it out. We would rather sweep it under the carpet and hope no one notices. Yet it will not go away. Time does not heal conflict, only resolution can do that. Conflict can be messy; it can be tiresome; it can be exhausting; and it can be embarrassing. I know from my own experience that conversations can haunt me for days; I can have sleepless nights; my mind will turn to the situation at a moment's notice and distract me endlessly. It is emotionally, psychologically, physically and spiritually draining. Yet, people are people. Those committed to ministry and to achieving tasks in the close confines of a team will experience conflict. The question should not be, 'How do we avoid conflict?' but 'How do we manage and resolve conflict?'

## Fighting fair

It is important, in the initial stages, that conflict is handled in such a way that it focuses attention on the principles or preferences at stake and not the individual personalities involved. It may become obvious over time, that the conflict may be more about a clash of personalities than about goals or aims. Nevertheless, in the early stages it is right to assume the best about those involved. In *When Caring Is Not Enough: Resolving Conflicts through Fair Fighting*, David Augsburger suggests that:

I can be right without finding you wrong.

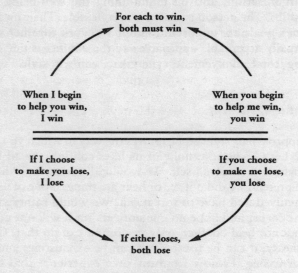

*Figure 16. Fair Fighting*[5]

You can be right without judging me wrong.
We may differ in fact, but not in act.
We may disagree on a problem, but not on the process.
We may fight about the content, but not damage the context.
The fight issue does not dictate the fight style.
The 'what' does not control the 'how'.[6]

## Asking the right question

In the midst of a conflict situation, it is all too easy to place ourselves in a self-justifying mode. Our emotions have been stirred. Things have been said and done. We feel that we have been 'hard done by'. We can be working in a charged atmosphere in which relationships are strained. Without too much effort, we can quickly start to question the other person's emotional stability, personality formation and spirituality! However, it is also vital to stop and to ask ourselves some searching questions too. It is good to first search our own hearts and to question our own motives, before we do it of others. As Jesus himself asked:

> Why do you look at the speck of sawdust in you brother's eye and pay no attention to the plank in your own eye? How can you say to your brother, 'Let me take the speck out of your eye,' when all the time there is a plank in you own eye? You hypocrite, first take the plank out of your own eye, and then you will see clearly to remove the speck from your brother's eye. (Matt. 7:3–5)

## Key questions

I have found three key questions have helped me to maintain both a healthy perspective of the total picture and to remain focused on the real issues.

1. 'What is the core issue at stake?'
2. 'Where am I wrong in my thinking?'
3. 'What are the possible solutions?'

David Augsburger lists ten questions which he maintains helps to maintain a sharp focus on the consequences of our own actions:

1. What is it, really, that is getting to me?
2. What is it, really, that I want to do about it?
3. What are the other options open to me?
4. What alternate ways of seeing, thinking, feeling are there?
5. What are the risks involved, the issues at stake?
6. What is the worst that could result from pressing the point?
7. What realistically do I really need, not just want?
8. How important is this change for me?
9. How difficult would this change be for the other?
10. How can I present my case so it can't be misunderstood?[7]

*Stepping stones*

Joyce Huggett, in her insightful book *Conflict: Friend or Foe?*
pinpoints a neglected but an important factor:

> If friction is to result in fruit-filled lives, we must allow it to
> be our teacher, the one who shows me where *I* need to grow
> in wholeness and maturity . . . We must allow it to be an
> umpire, one who sees that each person concerned stoops to
> servanthood without being reduced to a doormat. Certain
> questions will help us in the quest for creative conflict . . .
> They are irreplaceable stepping stones to conflict resolution:
>
> 1. What am I expecting from this fellowship/relationship?
> 2. What can I give to it?
> 3. Are my expectations realistic?
> 4. What do I appreciate about the person with whom I
>    am in conflict?
> 5. What is it about me that refuses to acknowledge the
>    good in them?
> 6. What is it about me that finds it hard to voice their
>    worth?
> 7. What is it about me that does not want to support them?
> 8. What is it about me that needs to change?
> 9. What is it about me that cannot cope with this relation-
>    ship?
> 10. Are we for each other or against each other?
> 11. Do we want this relationship to glorify God?
> 12. Is there something in me that is disrupting the unity of
>     God's people?
> 13. Lord, show me where I have failed. Bring me to the
>     place of repentance.[8]

These are searching questions which I would recommend that you
keep before you, particularly if you find yourself thinking very
negatively about the person or persons involved in the situation.
They have certainly been a significant help to me in times of
conflict. When embroiled in conflict, we do need to have our eyes
wide open in the situation, but at the same time, we still need to

see others through the eyes of Jesus. Whatever the rights and wrongs of the situation, it is vital that we take personal responsibility for being right before the Lord and maintaining a good relationship with him.

# 9

# Team struggles

In the midst of conflict it is sometimes all too easy to be so absorbed or distracted by the situation that you lose sight of what is actually happening. In other words you can't see the wood for the trees. Sometimes taking a step back and looking at the total picture can be a great help. If you focus away from the daily detail and focus on the complete scenario, the realism of what is actually happening can be the stimulus you need to take the necessary steps to resolve what is taking place and so work towards a reconciliation.

Some years ago when I was in the core of a conflict situation with a member of the pastoral team, I came across something that made me stop and take notice. The situation I was experiencing was so clearly painted that I could not miss it nor ignore it. It was the jolt I needed. It brought me to face the reality of what I really knew was happening but had been reluctant to face and resolve. Beyond that, I was given hope. A way out through what seemed like a jungle of confusion was plotted for me.

When a person is in the midst of an unresolved conflict it can sometimes seem like a bad dream at best or a nightmare at worst. Conflict can certainly cause many a sleepless night or a fretful waking in the early hours. Your mind is whirring away, going over and over all that has been said and done. The only difference is that you now have the perfect riposte and comment which somehow eluded you in the heat of the battle! With such a fretful mind and in such a bemused state you often end up asking yourself, 'Can this really be happening to me? This is just some bad dream. I will surely wake up and it will all be over!'

Being immersed in the painful reality of unresolved conflict can be a dark and lonely experience. Unfortunately conflict is not a dream from which we awake and discover our problems resolved and vanished like the early morning mist. If only life were that simple! What is more, unresolved conflict not only does not disappear, it also escalates over time. Like the dust swept away under the carpet, it does not go away and if left long enough produces ridges and bumps over which we have to carefully step as we walk on in our relationships.

## When it all falls apart

David Cormack observes that there are three major phases in the development of conflict which he plots on a 'Strife Curve'.[1]

### Phase 1. Separation

The parties involved initially emphasise the differences between

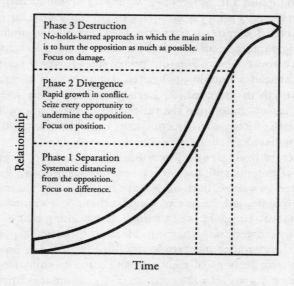

Figure 17. The Strife Curve[2]

themselves. The areas of disagreement are debated, discussed, argued over, etc. Sometimes the seedbed for conflict appears to have such an innocuous beginning but if resolution is not introduced at this preliminary stage then there can be a hardening of attitudes. The focus of people is to maintain their differences by drawing a line in the sand. Positions have been adopted, sides have been taken. People may even paint themselves into a corner by maintaining a particular stance. Emotions may begin to run high and others may be pulled into the fray. A systematic distancing from those who are perceived as the opposition begins.

## Phase 2. Divergence

At the end of the first phase, conflict as such has not really begun. This second phase marks the point when the parties involved seek to strengthen their own position and increasingly ignore any common ground or similarity with the person they now perceive as the enemy. There is a reluctance to work at resolving the presenting issues and differences. Whatever action or attitude the other person may adopt is now viewed from a particular negative perspective. Instead of thinking the best about them, they increasingly interpret all they do by imagining the worst. Even past events are now reviewed and interpreted from this new perspective. If these attitudes remain unchecked, then there is an inevitable rapid growth in the conflict. Each party will often seize every opportunity to undermine the other and so the distance between the parties is increased. The conflict is now becoming more open and recognisable.

Suspicions begin to arise, rumours may spread. Yet even during this phase there is still a superficial semblance of unity. Indeed in the context of a team, both outwardly and inwardly, a united front is often maintained. People will admit that there are differences, issues that are being worked through, but nothing that cannot be eventually sorted out. Beyond all the superficial posturing, however, undercurrents start to develop. In order to bolster the person's own feelings of rightness and sense of injustice, others begin to be drawn into the conflict. The confidant is unwittingly given a very one-sided account of what has transpired. If their story remains unchallenged, the telling of it will only confirm the person in their course of conflict. It will only serve to reinforce their mistaken belief that they are indeed blameless and do not need to change; their cause is just and they will not back down gracefully. The truth of most conflict situations is that, of course, there needs to be give and take on both sides. Humility, love and openness, which need to be demonstrated, are often conspicuous by their absence.

## Phase 3. Destruction

This phase sees the parties locked in conflict, which is often open and undisguised. The pretence has gone, and it is a no-holds-barred approach in which the main aim is to hurt the opposition. The focus is now on inflicting as much damage on the other party as possible. The longer the conflict continues to escalate unchecked the more aggressive and openly destructive the parties involved become towards each other. The longer the conflict continues, the more insensitive the people involved become. They may have begun with high moral words and principles, but soon *any* action becomes justifiable. Conflict not only destroys people, it also destroys their values.

If conflict remains unchallenged and unresolved, and those involved are left to themselves, then conflict tends to move up the 'Strife Curve'. As it does so, the parties will increasingly inflict more damage on themselves and on those around them. The effect on team members, the team, the group, the church, the organisation can be devastating. Even after the dust has settled, it can be like collecting an unravelled ball of string. Too much has been said and done. People have heard only one-sided accounts, part-truths and biased reports. Rumours and even gossip abound. Most people will probably never have the benefit of hearing the full story or being given all the pertinent facts. Besides which, many are no longer neutral dispassionate observers; they have been drawn into the emotions of the fray and so they too now view events past, present and even future, through prejudiced eyes. In church life and ministry, only the grace of God and the work of his Spirit in our lives can truly restore 'what the locusts have eaten' (Joel 2:25–9).

## Putting it back together again

If you are walking in a long dark tunnel and you eventually see a light at the other end, it could be either bad news or good news! It could be caused by a train coming towards you with its headlight on! Or it could be that you are approaching the end of the tunnel! So it is with conflict. Eventually a light will appear at the end of the tunnel. The light will either spell disaster, if nothing is being done to resolve the conflict, or the light will signal hope for a new day, a new beginning, as the process of resolving the conflict is worked through. David Cormack observes that there are three phases in the process of the 'Reconciliation Curve'.[3]

### Phase 1. Disengagement

The first step is to acknowledge what is occurring, its destructive nature, and to have a willingness to begin the journey of reconciliation. This step of 'disengagement' is often initiated by one party, which involves some measure of risk and humility. In taking the first step, and in doing it sensitively, they are giving a signal to the other party that they, at the very least, are admitting to some measure of blame and responsibility for what is happening. In a team or a leadership situation, the leader should give the lead and be willing to take the initiative and by example set a new direction. Hopefully, this will lead both parties to the point where they are prepared to 'call a cease-fire.'

A truce is a step beyond a cease-fire for it moves people one more step back from the brink. A cease-fire indicates the absence of hostilities, what we will not do; whereas a truce indicates the positive step of searching for agreement, the willingness to withdraw and step back from further confrontation. This vital step is often the hardest for many to make. Attitudes may have become entrenched and it becomes hard to back down and appear to give ground. Sometimes the weariness of the conflict forces it upon us. Sometimes external circumstances dictate that we stop. Pressure from peers, friends or colleagues may force the decision upon us.

Occasionally, the Spirit of God brings about the conviction that we are living a lie! There is a heaviness in our walk with the Lord

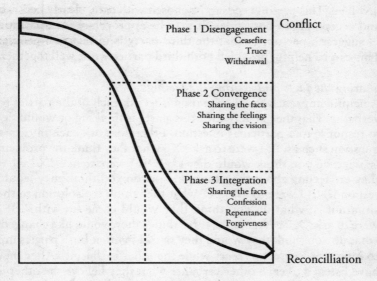

Figure 18. The Reconciliation Curve[4]

as we face up to the harsh fact that we are not walking in the light with another brother or sister in the Lord. Whatever the means, progress has been made towards the process of resolving the conflict and being reconciled with the other person.

## Phase 2. Convergence

During any conflict, one of the key areas that understandably suffers is that of communication. Mistrust, misunderstanding, suspicion and hurt cause people to withdraw into a safe shell out of earshot, away from the sound of the other. Conflict, as we have already noticed, causes people to hear and see only what they want to hear and see. It is crucial, therefore, for healthy and open communication to be re-established; people need to learn how to listen to one another again. They also need to learn how to talk to one another again. This is one of the most critical steps in the process to recovery.

A third party can sometimes be of great benefit to those

involved. This person needs to be chosen with care, clearly neutral, and acceptable to both sides. It may be appropriate for each side to suggest a person, so that the third party is in fact two people. This can be helpful provided both third parties work well together.

## Sharing the facts and sharing the feelings

A helpful approach that I have used is to ask each of the parties to verbalise what they believe the other party is thinking or would say in response to a particular question. I therefore ask each in turn a question such as, 'If I were to ask "X" what they think the problem is, what do you think would they say?' 'If I were to ask "X" what they are feeling about the situation, how do you think they would respond?' 'If I were to ask "X" what they think the solution to the situation is, what do you think they would come up with?' 'If I were to ask "X" what are the three things they would like changed, what do you think they would they say?' I instruct both parties not to interrupt, correct or react while the other is sharing. After they have listened to each other verbalise what they believe the other is thinking and feeling, I then ask them to respond as to how accurate they have been. If necessary I get them to add or subtract anything. In this way, the vital process of establishing some of the facts and the attendant feelings can be heard by all concerned.

This process is often referred to as 'sharing the facts' and 'sharing the feelings'. It must be remembered that even after a short time-spell of conflict, let alone one that has been going on for a long time, it is not just the facts that need to be resolved, but feelings have also been stirred. It is often the willingness to face these feelings and extend forgiveness which can be the determining factor as to whether there will be a successful reconciliation.

## Sharing the vision

This may result in the redressing of workloads, perhaps the re-writing of job descriptions, or the reassignment of responsibilities. Certainly the lines of authority and communication need to be agreed by all and spelt out clearly. This is referred to as 'sharing the vision', when both parties should be prepared to agree to steps that they will implement and take in the future.

Whatever is agreed, I strongly suggest that all agreements should be put in writing and copies given to both parties, including the third parties, for future reference. It is amazing how time can fog the issues and cloud the memories! This is an important point of closure, particularly if the parties have agreed to implement certain changes. It is a simple but effective way that will help all those concerned keep to their part of the agreement. It should also ensure an effective and lasting reconciliation.

## Phase 3. Integration

The main Greek word found in the New Testament for reconciliation is the verb *katallasso* and the noun *katallage*. The root meaning is 'to change from enmity and hostility to friendship'. It suggests that reconciliation is more than simply coming to an agreement but the restoring of the original relationship. Reconciliation is a process and will not occur instantly but rather evolves over time and involves the steps of confession, repentance and forgiveness.

These essential steps are needed to ensure that the once distant parties are truly brought close together. It is rare in conflict, if not impossible, to find the so-called innocent party and the so-called guilty party. Both parties must share and own the responsibility for what has taken place. It is usually six of one and half-a-dozen of the other. There are times when one party may have contributed the lion's share of maintaining the conflict, but even in those circumstances, confession, repentance and forgiveness is still appropriate for all concerned.

It must also never be peace at any price and the papering-over of the cracks. Reconciliation can be costly to all concerned. It is never easy to admit we are wrong, that we have been at fault, that we need to ask forgiveness. It is even harder to let go of hurt and to extend forgiveness when we feel we have been wronged. There is something in the human psyche, even among Christians and Christian leaders, in spite of all we preach and believe, which finds it hard to forgive and forget.

We discover to our shame that it is all too easy to harbour grudges, hold on to resentments and foster unforgiveness. Letting go does not come naturally or easily. Only those who have been through the heat of conflict know that it is truly costly to forgive from the heart. When both parties, however, stop to consider the high price of continuing the conflict, the price of reconciliation can seem to be a bargain not to be missed!

## When it is time to part

It is possible to go through the whole process and phases described above and yet still feel uneasy in the relationship. We need to be realistic as well as idealistic about team ministry. Perhaps too much has been said and done. Maybe mistakes have been made and the consequences are too hard or too painful to face every day. A fresh start is what is genuinely needed for all concerned. Perhaps, the common vision to which all felt so committed, because of all that has transpired, does not now draw that same commitment. The conflict, if achieving nothing else, may have at least clarified the small print of the vision.

### Incompatibility

It may of course be much more straightforward and a couple of team members are simply not compatible. Their temperaments, personalities, approach to life and ministry consistently produce tension and conflict and so bring out the worst rather than the best in each other. Try as they may there is a constant clash. This can be hard to admit or come to terms with, particularly for Christians. It is not always possible, even with the best will in the world, to get along with everybody. There are some people with whom we find it impossible build a close working relationship.

Is this an admission of failure? Is it evidence of a lack of spirituality? Is it a sign of inflexibility? Well, it might be! It may also be that a realistic recognition that we are all different, and that sometimes our differences, rather than enhancing a relationship, can detract from it. Rather than bringing out the best in people, they can bring out the worst in people. To apply Johnson and Johnson's concept of 'animal instincts', it is sometimes a case of not being able to teach an old dog new tricks or getting the leopard to change his spots. Let's be honest: sometimes it is hard to mix confirmed bears, owls, foxes, turtles and sharks in the same cage!

The majority of people in our society are married or are in some form of committed relationship. Even with a high divorce rate, and all the emotional trauma that produces, people would still rather be living with someone, rather than living on their own. The incidence of those being married, divorced and then remarried is extremely high. But even with all the societal and emotional pressure, there are still those who prefer to remain single. We should not be unnecessarily suspicious of these people but acknowledge that they prefer to live that way. In fact they would argue that they function more effectively with the added freedom their lifestyle affords them. The same observation can be made on occasions with those in team ministry.

I believe in marriage as an institution ordained by God to which most people will be called. I also believe there is a call to celibacy, of being single, to which some people are clearly called. The apostle Paul was such a person and he makes a very cogent case for such a lifestyle (1 Cor. 7). The same can be true of some people in ministry. For reasons of the nature of their temperament, personality, background, upbringing, experiences of life, etc., they find it uncommonly hard to settle into the discipline and challenges of a team ministry. I would also add that there are certain ministries in which a person can be more fruitful and effective if they minister on their own rather that in a team.

## Parting – such sweet sorrow

Whatever the reason, those involved may come to recognise that it is time to part. As Shakespeare observed, 'Parting is such sweet sorrow.' It is vitally important for all concerned that they part peacefully, and that they part reconciled. Escaping from the situation with matters unresolved, brings neither peace nor reconciliation. It is one thing to bury the past, but it must be buried dead and not buried alive, otherwise the spectre from the past will continue to haunt similar relationships in the future. A person should feel free to walk away from a team, the situation resolved and reconciled; wiser, enriched and more mature by the experience.

A person should, however, never run away from a team. I have observed that when they do, they inevitably take with them the baggage of the past. Eventually, yet certainly, their baggage will all be unpacked in the next situation, and the next, and the next. They will go round and round the same loop all over again, until they resolve to be reconciled with the past. We are all products of the past and so it is vital that, after any conflict, the past is dead and buried. In those circumstance it is all right to walk away, for we walk away in peace and in reconciliation – at peace with the past, and reconciled with those with whom we have struggled.

*Figure 19. Working Together*⁵

# Teamwork

As a pastor, I have noticed that when a person suspects that they might be seriously ill, they do not always respond in what others might observe as a logical manner. They will often denote the presence of the early tell-tale symptoms. They will refuse to go and see their doctor. They will carry on life as if all is well. There is, of course, a logical explanation to their behaviour. It may be because they cannot accept the possibility of being ill: 'This can't be happening to me!' Sometimes it is because it is inconvenient to admit they are ill: 'I have too much to do, I am too busy to be ill!' At other times it is because the person is naturally afraid. They cannot face the consequences of what the illness might entail: 'I can't face cancer! I can't go through the treatment!' These are understandable reactions to the inner turmoil caused by a serious illness.

Suppose they take the step and go to their doctor. He diagnoses what their illness is, and then sits back and says, 'I'm afraid there is nothing I can do for you!' That would be devastating news for the person. They know they are ill. They have come to the place of admitting it to themselves. The doctor knows they are ill. He can see and describe all the symptoms clearly, but he can do nothing for them. Today thankfully, doctors can do something for most illnesses.

In any close relationship, whether personal, working or pastoral, whether in marriage or in ministry, there will inevitably be tensions. If you have ever stood beside the place where two mountain streams merge and marvelled at the sound and energy of the surging, foaming, crashing waters then it should not surprise you that when two individuals, like living streams, merge into one that conflict occurs. Conflict, as we have already noted, is normal and natural; it is the denial of it or the avoidance of dealing with it that causes so many problems. The psychiatrist Eric Fromm says that 'Man would rather flee than fight.' Most of us when faced with conflict would rather turn the other way, embarrassed by the sight of it, uncertain as to what will become of it. We tend to equate avoiding the issues as keeping the peace and promoting harmony. We don't want to hurt or be hurt so we pretend all is well. Christians particularly can be slow to admit the presence of conflict, which they often view as a failure to love one another.

No relationship can exist very long without disappointments in a person's expectations of another. We are all sinners with different habits, attitudes, thoughts and values. These differences can then become the seedbed for conflict. Conflict can be like a cancer which grows inside a person. It may take time before a person is willing to admit how serious the situation is. It may take some time before they seek help. A person may recognise the symptoms but what is the cure?

## The cycle of conflict

Conflict is like going round and round in circles. If we grasp this fact, then we can break its hold over us and be set free from its gravitational pull. It is rare for conflict to be sustained aggression over a long period of time. It usually comes and goes. Richard Walton, in his book *Interpersonal Peacemaking*, observes that conflict between individuals is usually cyclical. At times the conflict will lie dormant, only to flare up in aggression and then die down again.

Conflict can be caused by substantive or attitudinal issues which can be suppressed for a long time – months, sometimes even years. Something or someone will trigger the person's response and cause the latent underlying conflict to flare up and rise to the surface. This triggering event will lead to a conflict issue becoming apparent. The trigger will cause a noticeable response and probably a reaction of conflict behaviour. Inevitably, conflict behaviours have knock-on effects. The roots, shoots and offshoots

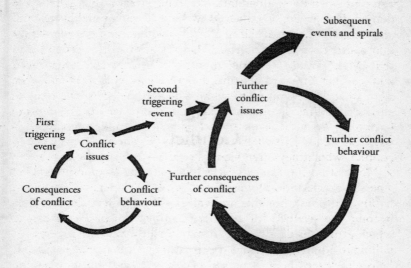

*Figure 20. The Spiral of Conflict¹*

of conflict can be very far-reaching and very damaging, even for innocent bystanders. Someone has wittily put it, 'When two elephants fight, the grass gets flattened!'

The conflict, having flared up, even if unresolved, will die down. But do not be deceived, it does not disappear. It sits hovering under the surface, until another trigger event fires it off again. So the cycles continue, except for a notable difference, the longer the cycles are left unresolved and unreconciled, the more they increase in intensity. As each issue is layered upon the previous ones, so the conflict builds in size and in its capacity to be destructive.

### Going round in circles

Conflict is a cycle which increases in size as time goes by, like some gigantic snowball gathering more snow as it plunges down the hill. Conflict is also a spiral which spins down into a deep vortex; its gravitational pull becoming stronger and more destructive as time goes by. This is because destructive behaviour forms a habit pattern

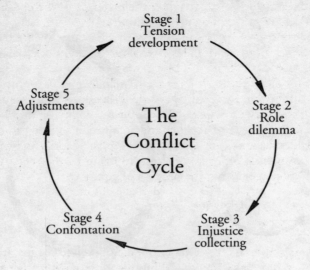

*Figure 21. The Conflict Cycle*[2]

which is hard to break. The longer the cycle remains unbroken the tighter the spiral will spin, and the stronger the vortex will become. This spiralling will not only increase in intensity, but also in frequency. The vicious circle, never-ending cycle and spinning spiral needs to be broken. The way out is to understand the structure of the cycle. The secret lies in understanding what causes the spiral to spin.

Norman Shawchuck has adapted the illustration of the 'Conflict Cycle' suggested by Robinson and Clifford, and maintains that once conflict begins it follows a five-stage progression. The length of any one stage may be very short (a few minutes) or very long (several months or years). All stages in the cycle are usually present.

I have found this cycle enormously helpful. An understanding of this cycle can be a significant key to unlocking the trap of conflict. It was of particular help to me personally some years ago in helping to work through what seemed like an intractable conflict situation with another pastor on our team. Its principles were a beacon of light in the darkness, a true light at the end of the tunnel. It enabled me to identify the issues at stake, the progress of the conflict and the difficulties in reaching a resolution.

Over the years I have made use of this cycle in a variety of pastoral situations, both in my own church and in other churches. I have used it in counselling married couples; in mission organisations; in leadership teams; in management groups; in task groups and so on. It has often provided the decisive help and been the defining factor which has enabled a team or a couple to recognise their cycle of conflict and so allow resolution to occur.

In the light of my own experiences, I have adapted Shawchuck's model to include other key factors to bring further clarity as to what takes place during the process of conflict.

## The tension mounts

Tension is a natural consequence of all close relationships. It is part and parcel of being human and mixing closely with other human beings. Something is said or done which is misplaced or misunderstood. A person reacts badly to a harmless but untimely comment. A cutting remark is made which wounds. An inappropriate observation is given which hurts. A person is under pressure and they displace their frustration on those around them. An insensitive word echoes in a person's mind. An over-sensitive person reads too much into what they think others may be saying. A person's hard work is taken for granted. A person is overlooked when the bouquets are handed out. A mistake is made, the ball is dropped, the assignment is blown. An assumption is made which remains unchallenged. A line of communication is ignored. An agreed procedure is by-passed. Inappropriate behaviour is noticed. Liberties are being taken by someone. Whatever the reason, an awkwardness is present, there is tension in the air. It can be so tense that it can be felt. People may even remark, 'You can cut the air with a knife!'

Some people spot tension straight away, while others do not, or if they do, they ignore it. In both cases, those concerned may do nothing to clear the air. It may be because those involved feel too embarrassed to mention the incident. They feel awkward at raising the situation. It is all too easy to turn and look the other way and

158

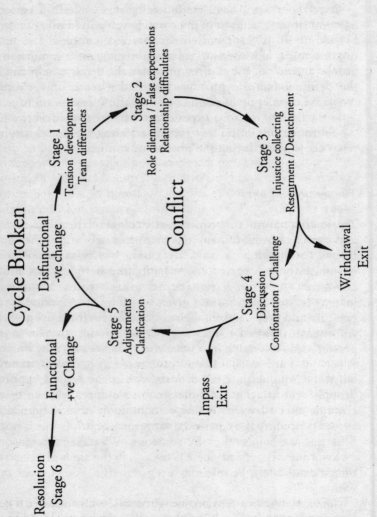

Figure 22. Working Model for Resolving Conflicts

**Cycle Broken**

**Conflict**

Stage 1
Tension development
Team differences

Stage 2
Role dilemma / False expectations
Relationship difficulties

Stage 3
Injustice collecting
Resentment / Detachment

Withdrawal
Exit

Stage 4
Discussion
Confrontation / Challenge

Impass
Exit

Stage 5
Adjustments
Clarification

Disfunctional
-ve change

Functional
+ve Change

Resolution
Stage 6

pretend nothing has really happened. Perhaps they feel it is too insignificant or petty to draw to the person's attention. Maybe they have been hurt and they feel too defensive to admit it. Perhaps the person finds it hard to admit their mistake, to apologise to those involved. Unfortunately the harmony of the relationship has now been dented. Uncertainty has crept into the situation. There is an awkwardness present below the surface. People can now become distanced from one another. The above is true for any team: a married couple; for those in an office; for business colleagues; for those on a leadership team; for members of a pastoral team.

Tensions should be recognised, acknowledged and resolved as quickly as possible. Situations should not be allowed to drift. We have noticed that team members need to keep short accounts with others in order to stay spiritually sharp and keep their cutting edge in ministry. If a mistake is made it should be admitted and where appropriate forgiveness and reconciliation should be sought. If a person steps out of line they should be challenged and when necessary, they should apologise for their action.

Most conflicts begin at the very basic humdrum level of life. The nickel and dime incidents, if left unpaid, can mount up to cost big bucks down the road. It is a universal observation that the fifteen most difficult words to pronounce in the English language are: 'I am sorry! I am wrong! You are right! Please forgive me! I appreciate you!' On the other hand, a person may need just as much courage to question an action or an attitude which they detect in another person. To state the obvious: tension in any kind of team will dissipate if it is dealt with at the earliest opportunity. People are different, and that requires adjustments to be made. Strong and lasting relationships are built on the firm foundation of honesty and integrity between team members.

## Right relationships

Tension arising between people working closely together, if ignored or inadequately dealt with, will inevitably lead to poor relationships between people. It is vital to keep short accounts with those with whom we work. Sometimes it is simply a matter of developing a deeper understanding and rapport with others; taking time to listen and to share in their joys and successes, their struggles and challenges. If a team is too task-orientated then relationships will remain superficial and can appear to be sacrificed on the altar of achieving the overarching goal. Time and sensitivity need to be given to unearth and bring to the surface any unresolved feelings or incidents from the past. An atmosphere needs to be generated that allows, and indeed gives permission, for any tensions that might be present to surface. This is not to encourage a digging-up of the dirt but to encourage a healthy removing of unresolved issues and incidents which the person may have buried but are still, nevertheless, very much alive.

Despite all our best efforts, we may come to the reluctant but inevitable conclusion that the person does not fit in. Other factors may effect the flow of relationships. Perhaps it is a personality clash; a divergent philosophy of ministry; an individualistic approach to life; a contrary view of ministry; an unwillingness to submit to the disciplines of being part of a team. People are unique so every team is unique, and everyone does not always make a perfect fit. Too big a difference may disqualify a person from fitting into a team. Occasionally, calling it quits may be the right way out for all concerned. Failure to do so may propel the team into a constant cycle of conflict.

## The right role

One of the prime causes for conflict in a team is role dilemma. A person is uncertain about their job description. Perhaps, their area of responsibility has not been clearly spelt out. Assumptions are made about what they should or should not do, or can and cannot do. A person can presume authority in a situation that is not theirs to exercise. The procedures of consultation or communication, which we examined earlier, have been ignored. The tell-tale signs of role dilemma are not difficult to spot. It can often lead to confusion as a person questions their own role or discovers others questioning what their role is.

In team ministry it is not unusual for this stage to become a point of contention. As people work together they discover fresh areas of interest. They become involved in different arenas of ministry and unknown abilities may surface. Sometimes in that process they may neglect their agreed assignments or tread on someone else's turf. A person may prefer to be doing something else, to have other responsibilities other than the ones for which they came on to the team. So almost imperceptibly they can subtly drift out of their own area and manoeuvre themselves into a new one. In a more sinister fashion, a person can harbour false ambitions and will take on assignments or additional responsibilities to prove their ability and so further their own ambitions.

The presence of tension is the warning light that the team is not functioning as it should. If it is ignored, possible danger and disaster lie ahead! From my experience of handling conflict within pastoral team ministry, this area is the seedbed of more conflict than anything else. In the conflict with an associate pastor, described in an earlier chapter, role dilemma was the prime cause of the conflict.

Resolution to the conflict was achieved through painstakingly exploring and clarifying both his role, as an associate pastor, and my role, as the senior pastor. On other occasions in the pastorate it has also been necessary to clarify a team member's role. Thus false assumptions, misunderstandings, and miscommunications can be laid to rest.

In talking with other pastors and team leaders, often the entry point for conflict and even division in a team has been through the initial questioning of role dilemma. This may have be done overtly or covertly. Looking back, people often regret not having broached the area earlier. The latent ambition, dissatisfaction or misunderstanding paved the way for future heart-searching and heartbreaking conflict. All leaders will agree that it is not always an easy area to sort through. It is, however, vital if the future health and strength of the team and its members are to be maintained.

## Sense of injustice

If the cycle remains unchecked and unchallenged then the door to injustice collecting is opened. If the causes of team differences and the resultant tension have not been explored openly and honestly, then the tension will increase to the point that communication between people begins to break down. The differences between the other team member or the team leader are now viewed as intolerable. Those involved may be covertly or even overtly blaming each other. At moments of frustration, there have been a few exchanges along the way but nothing has really been worked through. There is a disruptive and undermining influence at work in the team. This is a dangerous stage to be at. Those involved are usually convinced that matters can now only get worse. Hope has dwindled that the situation will right itself. There is a sinking feeling of what may lie ahead.

Those involved begin to pull apart and view others not only as simply different to them but actively working against them. They view the whole situation from a quite different perspective. They now see themselves as opponents who are preparing for battle which they are convinced will take place sooner or later. It is, therefore, essential to have ammunition and artillery with which to fight the battle and defeat the enemy. The original issue which caused the tension and precipitated the conflict will now not only be remembered, but also added to.

Notes may be made of conversations, details kept of specific grievances. Copies of letters sent and received are carefully kept. Each item of injustice is now preserved and catalogued, if not in actuality, certainly in the mind and heart. Each further incident is layered on to the previous ones. Every situation and motive is no longer viewed dispassionately, but is viewed through the grid of grievance and the narrow lens of suspicion. The result is that those involved convince themselves, beyond doubt, that they have reasonable grounds to confirm their position and refute that of the other person. They are ready to do battle.

Injustice collecting sows the seeds of resentment, bitterness, unforgiveness and a self-righteousness which is easy to understand for anyone who has been involved in close conflict. However, understandable as it may be, it is not easy to equate with the Spirit of God at work in a person's life, particularly if that person is in a position of spiritual leadership. It needs, therefore, with the grace of God, to be resisted, changed and stopped.

## Resolution

If conflict is to be resolved, then those involved have to be prepared to discuss head-on what is happening. They have to be prepared to challenge attitudes and actions, to be willing to confront the problems they face together. The very word confrontation has a negative connotation for many. It conjures up a bitter, violent and intractable situation in which both parties are at each other's throats. This is understandable, because so often the word is used by the media of radio and television to convey a deadlocked embittered battle between two belligerent parties.

*Chambers Dictionary* defines confrontation simply as 'bringing people face to face'.[3] So, confrontation, in and of itself, need not necessarily be negative. Confrontation is the willingness to discuss and to deal with the issues involved. We have to be realistic, however, and recognise that if conflict exists between people, then the act of 'bringing people face to face' can release negative emotions, reactions and responses. This can be difficult and painful to handle and sometimes even to control.

Nevertheless, for the tension, the sense of injustice and the conflict to be dealt with, then confrontation is the only way forward. Those in disagreement need to be brought together. Sometimes, one of those involved may take the initiative; perhaps they are the team leader or in a position of leadership or management. If this is done at an early enough stage, or in an early cycle in the spiral, then it can bring the conflict to a successful conclusion. If the conflict has been taking place over a long period of time and has run deep, then a third party may be necessary to help in the process. We looked at ways in which this can be done in an earlier chapter.

Beyond the timing of the confrontation and those involved in the process, there is a far more important factor. The attitude in which the confrontation is handled will probably be the determining factor as to whether it is successful or not. Shawchuck makes this astute observation: 'Confront not in hostility, not through the power of your position, but in love. Meet each other, sit down, talk, listen, consult one another. Enemies will be enemies until they talk to each other.'[4]

He makes the following helpful comments concerning the process of conflict management and confrontation: 'Keep everyone focused on the conflict issues. As conflict progresses people tend to forget the issue which started the conflict in the first place. They become angry and turn away from the issue to fighting each other.'[5]

Shawchuck lists his three 'P's' of conflict management:

1. Permission: Give the parties permission to disagree without feeling guilty.
2. Potency: Enable each one to state his/her position with strength and clarity.
3. Protection: Keep each one from being needlessly hurt, and from needlessly hurting the other.[6]

It needs to be said that the process of confrontation does not always break the cycle of conflict. There can be a number of reasons for this. The focus of attention may stray from the underlying issues and be focused on surface causes. The real heart issues, the foundational causes, are therefore never dealt with. Those involved may spend the time justifying their own positions and placing blame on the other person, rather than working together towards a solution. The process itself may not be managed well. However, beyond these observations, there is a much more fundamental reason why often the conflict cycle is not broken.

## Making the changes

People need to make changes to end conflict. It is not simply a question of making some adjustments. It is the right adjustments that need to be made. If the cycle and spiral of conflict are to be broken, then it is those adjustments which will bring a lasting resolution which need to be made. Unfortunately, it is not unusual to find people making changes which do not amount to much more than tinkering with the engine, rather than a major overhaul.

If the right adjustments are made, they will have a positive effect on the situation and will lead to a functional resolution of the conflict. They need to be not only the right changes, but they also need to be implemented. It is one thing for people to agree to change, it is often quite another matter for them to implement it. Any agreed adjustments should be put in writing and then circulated to all those involved in the conflict and confrontation process. The failure to implement agreed adjustments is one of the prime reasons why conflicts are not resolved. The lack of implementation of agreed adjustments will result in the cycle and spiral tightening and continuing.

The frustration caused by lack of progress, following the time and energy of the confrontation process, will usually cause an increase in the dimension of the cycle and in the tightness of the spiral. Those involved will also be more reluctant to enter the confrontation process the next time round. After all, they will say, 'It did not do any good!' 'So-and-so is as bad as ever, he hasn't changed a bit.' 'Things are even worse than before!' What is more, those involved will probably be more intransigent during any future confrontation and reconciliation processes.

## Implementation

Implementation also involves the willingness of those involved to be challenged by others if they cross the boundaries of agreed territory; if they step over the line in a given area; if they do not keep their particular part of the bargain. For example, one of the adjustments may be that an associate pastor agrees to the priority and importance of pastoral team meetings. He agrees to attend all scheduled meetings; not to arrange any other meetings to clash with that time, to be punctual in arriving and not to leave early.

All may go well for several weeks. The day he skips a meeting, arrives late or has to leave early is the day he must be challenged. He must be held to his agreed adjustment. Failure to do so immediately will usually cause an inexorable slip back into tension development and so back into the conflict cycle. The adjustments may be agreed in a day, but they need to be worked out over several months to ensure that they become functional and keep the reconciliation in place.

Positive functional adjustments are the changes that are needed, that are agreed, and that are implemented. They will pave the way to a lasting resolution of the conflict. They will break the remorseless cycle and spiral of conflict.

Negative dysfunctional adjustments are the changes that are needed but are not implemented. They may be the changes that are agreed, but are not needed to resolve the issues. They may be the changes that are agreed but not implemented. The result is that the conflict is not resolved. The parties may make peace, but they are not reconciled. Tension will creep back into the relationship, which if unchallenged and unresolved will then recreate the cycle.

### Honourable withdrawal or swift exit

In the working model for resolving conflict there are two points leading away from the cycle. The first is after 'injustice collecting'. A person may get to the place in which they feel nothing will ever change or be done about the situation. They may then 'exit' the team. Sometimes these exits can be sudden, dramatic and unexpected. They will leave following a disagreement which is seen as the last straw. A person may resign and move on apparently right out of the blue or they may not so much exit, as 'withdraw'. The person perhaps suspects that the crunch is coming because the possibility of a confrontation has been mentioned. Maybe the person cannot face that or they feel that they will be made out to be the villain of the piece, so they make an honourable withdrawal.

Perhaps the person cannot face the consequences of being challenged or confronted with some of their behaviour. They want to avoid having to deal with deeper personal issues which will surface. They may have a rebellious spirit which will not submit to others and which resists being challenged by others. Whatever the motive, for some 'exit' is the means to break away from the cycle.

The second alternative way out of the cycle follows the 'discussion' or 'confrontation'. The person may find that they cannot cope with the adjustments that are necessary. It may be that the confrontation has not been handled well, or it may be that they simply cannot handle or face up to the concept of change being needed in their life and relationships. They may therefore 'exit' the team. They will usually resign or leave as quickly as possible.

Alternatively, there will be an 'impasse'. The person refuses to change and blames all and sundry for the conflict – all that is except for themselves. They refuse to accept the adjustments that are necessary. Even with the help of a third party, it becomes clear that an impasse has been reached. In this instance they may have to be gently encouraged to leave. Sometimes they dig in their heels and they have to be asked or even told to leave.

## Aftermath

Whenever a person leaves, either as a result of 'withdrawal', 'exit' or an 'impasse', the underlying conflict usually remains unresolved. Part of the problem may have moved on, but the personal and team issues remain behind. The tragedy is, particularly for Christians, especially those in leadership, that relationships may be left unreconciled. There may be the residue of resentment, bitterness and unforgiveness. We have already noticed that time does not heal these emotions, only forgiveness and reconciliation. The baggage a person takes with them when they leave one team will inevitably be unpacked on to future teams. They may have to reap the consequences of unresolved past conflict.

## Closing the circle

The 'conflict cycle' is also a great tool to help in initial team building. I advise every team leader to give a full explanation of it in the early stages of team building, although it is never too late to introduce it, even in an established team. The recognition that conflict is neutral, normal and natural will be of great relief and help to a team. It as an encouragement for people to know that tensions are inevitable when working closely together, even among spiritual people! The cause of those tensions and the way in which they are resolved are the key points to focus in on. Team members need to recognise that, under your leadership, conflict will not be avoided or denied. It will be dealt with honestly, quickly and biblically. Such an approach to the realities of team life will be a solid plank in team building. A straightforward attitude to conflict will augur well for the team's future health, strength and effectiveness.

The 'Prayer for Peace' by St Francis of Assisi puts it so well:

Lord make me an instrument of thy peace;
Where there is hatred, may I bring love;
Where there is injury, may I pardon;
Where there is discord, may I bring union;
Where there is error, may I bring truth;

Where there is doubt, may I bring faith;
Where there is despair, may I bring hope;
Where there is darkness, may I bring light;
Where there is sadness, may I bring joy.

Oh Master, make me not so much to be consoled as to
console;
Not so much to be loved as to love;
Not so much to be understood as to understand;
For it is in giving that one receives;
It is in self-forgetfulness that one finds;
It is in pardoning that one is pardoned;
It is in dying that one finds eternal life.

# II

# Team event

Throughout this book I have emphasised the fact that in ministry we need not be on our own. God's pattern for ministry is team ministry, in all its various forms. To corrupt the Scripture: 'It is not good for us to be on our own!' I now want to examine three different situations which illustrate this point. First, that of marriage; second, that of athletics; and third, that of steam.

## Walking the aisle

In our church we will not agree to conduct a wedding service unless the couple agree to meet with another Christian couple for five sessions and complete a 'preparation for marriage' course. We tell them that preparing for the wedding is important, but it is over in a day. What is more important is to prepare them for marriage, which will last a lifetime. We want people to go into marriage with their eyes wide open to all the exciting potential that awaits them. We want them to be appraised of some of the pitfalls that await the unwary and the unprepared; that they will experience the marital stages of 'enchantment', 'disenchantment' and 'maturity'.

Team ministry and being part of a team can sometimes feel like a marriage. The parallels are clearly to be seen. There is the courtship phase (the candidating); the announcement of the engagement (the hiring); the wedding (the induction/ordination service); and married life (the joys and tears of ministry)! The emotional trauma of leaving a team, whether for good reasons (moving on), or bad reasons (being fired/dehired), can feel like a bereavement or a divorce.

Perhaps for some, who are about to become part of a team or have just joined a team, this book has been a 'preparation for marriage' course! For others, who are veteran team members, the book is more akin to a 'marriage enrichment' seminar! Whatever your experience may be, it is important in team ministry not to have your head in the clouds, but to have your feet firmly on the ground.

A person does need to think twice before joining or leading a leadership team – whether that be pastoral, missionary, organisational or lay. Working closely with others will always require effort. It can be a rewarding and enriching time if relationships are positive and healthy. The experience, however, if relationships are strained, can be also be quite the opposite. This is not to discourage you, but make sure that you do your homework carefully and go in with your eyes wide open.

I have found each team to have been a unique and rich experience, with its own strengths and weaknesses. I have not been the same person in each team of which I have been a member. Teams are never static, there is always change, sometimes in membership, hopefully in maturity. I count myself fortunate, over twenty years of pastoral team ministry, to have been given the opportunity to serve on the teams of which I have been a member. They were not without difficulty and stress. As in all marriages there are times of tension and the temptation to quit and go elsewhere. Teamwork certainly does divide the effort and multiply the effect, but it does involve work to achieve that. Pastoral/ministry/leadership/missionary teams are not marriages made in heaven, but partnerships that God calls us to work in, for a limited time, to achieve his plans and purposes in us, for us and through us.

## It's a relay race

As a young man I was a keen and active track athlete. Although I competed primarily in middle distance events, I also loved to run the 400 meters, particularly as part of a four by 400 meters relay team. I was usually given the assignment of running the anchor leg. This event is traditionally the last event of the track meeting. I used to look forward to it because it was a team event. Most of my other races, even when representing my club or country were, nevertheless, solo efforts.

A relay race, whatever the distance, is a genuine team event. Even the best 1,500 meters runner cannot hope to beat his peers over four laps when the others are only running one lap each. Running on your own against others in a team is a recipe for losing. Teamwork has been defined as 'Working together means winning together.' So much more can be accomplished when people work together.

Relay races also generate enormous interest and enthusiasm from spectators and competitors alike. There was many a time I cheered myself almost hoarse through encouraging the lead-off runners on their way around the track. I had so lost myself in their performance that I had almost forgotten I too had to run my lap! Of course I did have a vested interest, because their leg of the relay, their performance, would effect the starting position of my leg and so possibly my own performance. Sometimes I felt an awesome responsibility, as I stood waiting to receive the baton from the incoming runner. I too wanted to run well and not let down those who had already given their all.

Team ministry takes many different forms: a pastoral staff; a board of deacons; an eldership; a missionary committee; an executive; a leadership group; a ministry task group; a missions project team; an organisational management group. Within those contexts it is possible to function as a solo performer. It is possible to be an athlete representing the team, but running alone around the track in our own chosen event. It is possible to have an attitude which may recognise and respect the other track athletes and appreciate the skill of their events, but which is distanced from them.

Teams of all descriptions need to recognise that as team members we are all taking part in the same event. We are running as part of the same relay team. We are competing in the same race. There is no other feeling to match the sense of achievement through competing and celebrating as a result of a team effort. We need to stand around the track and encourage each other as we each run our own leg of the relay. What a difference that can make to a person's performance. As the writer to the Hebrews puts it:

Since we are surrounded by such a great crowd of witnesses, let us throw off everything that hinders and the sin that so

easily entangles, and let us run with perseverance the race
marked out for us. Let us fix our eyes on Jesus, the author
and perfecter of our faith . . . Therefore, strengthen your
feeble arms and weak knees! (Heb. 12:1, 2, 12)

It has to be admitted though, that working closely together at full
speed is not always easy. It will always be a challenge for gifted competitors. Teams need to learn the difference between passing the
buck and passing the baton! Many teams are comprised of highly
talented individuals, chosen for the gifts and abilities, who find themselves grouped together in a team. Making a group of 'All-Stars'
into a true team can be quite a challenge for all concerned. This
book has endeavoured to show how a team can keep the momentum
moving, and yet still keep the exchanges smooth between the runners.

## Full S.T.E.A.M. ahead

It would be a mistake to think that all this can be achieved on our
own. Beyond all the human insights, effort and ingenuity we still
need more assistance. Once again we discover that we are not on
our own. Team, as we have noticed, can be defined as T.E.A.M.:
'Together Everyone Achieves More.' With the help of the Spirit of
God at work in their midst, a team can also add the all-important
spiritual dimension. An ordinary group of people, allowing God's
Spirit to work in them, can truly achieve more!

It is as God's Spirit works in individual team members, and then
through them, collectively as a team, that they will be transformed
into S.T.E.A.M. Steam is a powerful and effective force, whose
energy can be harnessed for good and for God. Steam is generated
by heat being applied to cold water. So it is with the Spirit of God.
The Spirit can take cold hearts and set them on fire with the love
of Jesus. This love will then motivate and drive people to live with
and for others. This fire will, in turn, empower them to be effective
in fulfilling the vision of the team and so their unique contribution
in extending the kingdom of God.

I am still as committed to the concept of team ministry as I was
the day I was ordained, in fact even more so. Over the years I have
matured in my understanding of, and belief in, team ministry. I still

remain undeniably optimistic about teams and hopelessly committed to team ministry. It is my firm conviction, from both my personal experience and the exposition of Scripture, that team ministry is the way a church or Christian organisation, should be led. This applies equally to a team of professional paid staff or lay volunteers or a mixture of both. In each team of which I have been a member, I have learnt invaluable lessons about ministry, about myself and about my God. Truly we are richer together and poorer apart!

### Team spirit

I have penned a creative adaptation of the 'Hymn of Love' from 1 Corinthians 13, based on an idea from David Cormack. It reads as follows:

If I can speak in the jargon of team ministry,
And if I can recite all management principles perfectly;
Yet if I lack team spirit,
My words are hollow and carry no weight.

And though I have vision and can set objectives,
Solve problems and analyse situations;
Yet if I am not motivated by team spirit,
I will achieve nothing.

And though I spend all my time and energy on behalf of others,
And burn myself out in the course of my effort;
Yet if I do all these things outside team spirit,
No one benefits.

For team spirit listens, it is patient and forgiving;
It is not boastful, forceful or ambitious.
Team spirit believes the best of others,
Team spirit wants the best for others,
Team spirit brings out the best in others.

As for all the management gurus,

One day they will be silent.
As for all the latest team techniques,
Soon they will be out-of-date.
A team depends on commitment, motivation and team spirit;
No team can survive without these three.
But the greatest of these is team spirit.

# Leadership Resources

176

# Entering the B zone by Ray and Anne Ortlund

Outline 1

Moses' project of getting his
fellow Hebrews out of Egypt

——— Enlarges into ———→

Project to govern
the escaped Hebrews
in righteousness

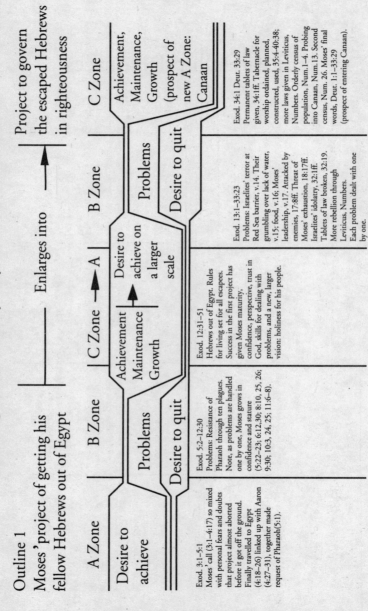

| A Zone | B Zone | C Zone → A | C Zone | B Zone | C Zone |
|---|---|---|---|---|---|
| Desire to achieve | Problems / Desire to quit | Achievement Maintenance Growth / Desire to achieve on a larger scale | Achievement Maintenance Growth | Problems / Desire to quit | Achievement, Maintenance, Growth (prospect of new A Zone: Canaan |

Exod. 3:1–5:1
Moses' call (3:1–4:17) so mixed with personal fears and doubts that project almost aborted before it got off the ground. Finally travelled to Egypt (4:18–26) linked up with Aaron (4:27–31), together made request of Pharaoh (5:1).

Exod. 5:2–12:30
Problems: Resistance of Pharaoh through ten plagues. Note, as problems are handled one by one, Moses grows in confidence and stature (5:22–23; 6:12,30; 8:10, 25, 26; 9:30; 10:3, 24, 25; 11:6–8).

Exod. 12:31–51
Hebrews out of Egypt. Rules for living set for all escapees. Success in the first project has given Moses maturity, confidence, perspective, trust in God, skills for dealing with problems, and a new, larger vision: holiness for his people.

Exod. 13:1–33:23
Problems: Israelites' terror at Red Sea barrier, v.14. Their grumbling over lack of water, v.15; food, v.16; Moses' leadership, v.17. Attacked by enemies, 17.8ff. Threat of Moses' exhaustion, 18.17ff. Israelites' idolatry, 32:1ff. Tablets of law broken, 32:19. More rebellion through Leviticus, Numbers. Each problem dealt with one by one.

Exod. 34:1 Deu. 33.29
Permanent tablets of law given, 34:1ff. Tabernacle for worship ordained, planned, constructed, used, 35:4–40:38; more laws given in Leviticus, Numbers. Orderly census of population, Num. 1–4. Probing into Canaan, Num. 13. Second census, Num. 26. Moses' final words, Deu. 1:1–33:29 (prospect of entering Canaan).

Outline 2
Nehemiah's project of
rebuilding Jerusalem's wall

Project to govern
the Transjordan
Jews in righteousness

Enlarges into

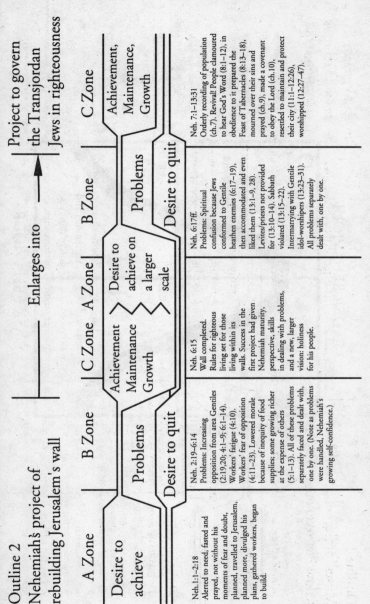

| A Zone | B Zone | C Zone | A Zone | B Zone | C Zone |
|---|---|---|---|---|---|
| Desire to achieve | Problems | Achievement Maintenance Growth | Desire to achieve on a larger scale | Problems | Achievement, Maintenance, Growth |
| | Desire to quit | | | Desire to quit | |

Neh.1:1–2:18
Alerted to need, fasted and prayed, not without his moments of fear and doubt, planned, travelled to Jerusalem, planned more, divulged his plans, gathered workers, began to build.

Neh. 2:19–6:14
Problems: Increasing opposition from area Gentiles (2:19,20; 4:1–9; 6:1–14). Workers' fatigue (4:10). Workers' fear of opposition (4:11–23). Lowered morale because of inequity of food supplies; some growing richer at the expense of others (5:1–13). All of these problems separately faced and dealt with, one by one. (Note as problems were handled, Nehemiah's growing self-confidence.)

Neh. 6:15
Wall completed. Rules for righteous living set for those living within its walls. Success in the first project had given Nehemiah maturity, perspective, skills in dealing with problems, and a new, larger vision: holiness for his people.

Neh. 6:17ff.
Problems: Spiritual confusion because Jews conformed to Gentile heathen enemies (6:17–19), then accommodated and even liked them (13:1–9, 28). Levites/priests not provided for (13:10–14). Sabbath violated (13:15–22). Intermarrying with Gentile idol-worshipers (13:23–31). All problems separately dealt with, one by one.

Neh. 7:1–13:31
Orderly recording of population (ch.7). Revival! People clamoured to hear God's Word (8:1–12), in obedience to it prepared the Feast of Tabernacles (8:13–18), mourned over their sins and prayed (ch.9), made a covenant to obey the Lord (ch.10), resettled to maintain and protect their city (11:1–12:26), worshipped (12:27–47).

# Situational Leadership Model by Paul Hersey and Kenneth Blanchard

**Decision styles**

1 Leader-made decision

2 Leader-made decision with dialogue and/or explanation

3 Leader/follower-made decision or follower-made decision with encouragement from leader

4 Follower-made decision

**LEADER BEHAVIOUR**

**3**

Share ideas and facilitate in decision making

High Rel. Low Task

**2**

Explain decisions and provide opportunity for clarification

HighTask Low Rel.

**4**

Turn over responsibility for decisions and implementation

Low Rel. Low Task

**1**

Provide specific instructions and closely supervise performance

High Task Low Rel.

Selling

Participating

Delegating

Telling

HIGH

**RELATIONSHIP BEHAVIOUR**
(Supportive Behaviour)

LOW

HIGH **TASK BEHAVIOUR**
(Guidance)

**Task Behaviour –**
The extent to which the leader engages in defining roles telling what, how, when, where, and if more than one person, who is to do what in:

• Goal-setting
• Organising
• Establishing time lines
• Directing
• Controlling

**Relationship Behaviour –**

The extent to which the leader engages in two-way (multi-way)communication, listening, socioemotional support

• Giving support
• Communicating
• Facilitating interactions
• Active listening
• Providing feedback

## Follower Readiness

| High | Moderate | | Low |
|------|----------|--|-----|
| R4 | R3 | R2 | R1 |
| Able and willing or confident | Able but unwilling or insecure | Unable but willing or confident | Unable and unwilling or insecure |

Follower Directed ———————————— Leader Directed

**Ability:**
Has the necessary knowledge, experience and skill

**Willingness:**
Has the necessary confidence, commitment and motivation

When a Leader Behaviour is used appropriately with its corresponding level of readiness, it is termed a High Probability Match. The following are descriptors that can be useful when using Situational Leadership for specific applications:

| S1 | S2 | S3 | S4 |
|----|----|----|----|
| Telling | Selling | Participating | Delegating |
| Guiding | Explaining | Encouraging | Observing |
| Directing | Clarifying | Collaborating | Monitoring |
| Establishing | Persuading | Commiting | Fulfilling |

# Pastoral Team Guidelines
# of Bramalea Baptist Church

### Objective:

To assist the healthy development of the pastoral team by setting down guidelines which will clarify expectations and define responsibilities. The intent is to set up a supportive structure to facilitate ministry and the effective functioning of the pastoral team.

1. *Positions covered:*

    1.1 All members of the pastoral team.

2. *Definition of the Pastoral Team*

    2.1 Those who are appointed by the church to exercise specific pastoral leadership.

    2.2 Those who are recognised for their gifting and called by God to give their time fully for the primary task of pastoral ministry.

    2.3 The leader of this team is the senior pastor.

    2.4 Other people may be members of this team (on a part time or voluntary basis).

    2.5 All appointments to the pastoral team to be approved by the senior pastor and the deacons in consultation with the pastoral team and church members as appropriate.

3. *Working of the Pastoral team*

A successful team is one in which there is mutual respect, regular and open communication.

3.1 The team is expected to meet together on a regular, probably weekly, basis for sharing and prayer.

3.2 The team will operate on an open diary basis where other members are aware of appointments and commitments (subject to the needs of confidentiality).

3.3 Any team member's absence from BBC (e.g. a day or more away) will be agreed with the senior pastor and in consultation with the other team members.

3.4 For their own health and welfare team members are not expected to work more than fifteen units per week. The unit consists of a morning, afternoon or evening.

3.5 An alternative way of calculating ministry input without burnout could be forty hours paid employment, six hours for Sunday services, and eight hours voluntary time. Any team member who consistently puts in over sixty hours per week would cause concern.

3.6 Monitoring of this would be part of the ministry and annual review process.

4. *Prayer*

The church relies on the pastors making time to pray and listen to God.

4.1 As well as having an active individual prayer-life and praying with other pastoral team members, it is expected that team members will participate in prayer retreats together each year.

## 5. Time for ministries outside BBC

We recognise the importance of giving a portion of the time and effort of the BBC pastoral team to the wider work of building the kingdom. It is a part of our kingdom work and a clear responsibility of BBC. We desire to provide boundaries within which the pastoral team can operate freely without causing problems for the church or their fellow members. Obviously this is not intended to restrict what a member does in their own time. Each member shall have a maximum percentage of their time which they may spend outside BBC.

5.1   'Inside' BBC are those things which extend the kingdom within the community of Brampton, Greater Metropolitan Toronto area and are within the BBC mission statement of worship, fellowship, mission, stewardship and discipleship.

5.2   'Outside' BBC is every activity which is not specifically BBC work except where specifically representing BBC.
      a) e.g. FEBCENTRAL meetings, local ministerial meetings, outside Board memberships, preaching away.
      b) these areas of activity would normally be established at a ministry review (see section 11), however, changes in these areas must be approved by the senior pastor and deacons board prior to commitments being made. For example, if a team member were asked to take on an outside board position, this would be discussed at the earliest opportunity. The deacons will approve the changes and the pastoral team will work out the details of them.

5.3   *Away time*
      The time will vary for each member of the pastoral team and should be agreed upon prior to joining the team. It will be reviewed at subsequent ministry reviews.

5.4   Any costs incurred in these outside ministries, not

covered by the outside work would need to be budgeted and agreed in the normal way.

5.5 In addition at any time, responding to a particular opportunity which could not have been foreseen, may be reconsidered by the deacon board.

6. *Attendance at services*

6.1 Team members are normally expected to be at all Sunday services even if they are not taking part. There needs to be some flexibility about this so that their gifts can be shared with others. Individual occasions will be agreed with the senior pastor before acceptance. The extent of this will be included in the ministry review as part of the outside time.

6.2 Any absence from Sunday services requires advance permission from the senior pastor.

7. *Reporting responsibility*

In order for the team to be effective, mutual accountability is important while recognising the role of the team leader.

7.1 Each of the team members is to report to the pastoral team meeting on a week-to-week basis and on a ministry review/appraisal basis to the senior pastor and deacons.

7.2 In the case of a dispute within the pastoral team the matter should be handled through the disputes procedures.

8. *Disputes procedures*

In a team of Christians working together there will be some tensions. It is expected that the vast majority of these will be resolved between the individuals concerned. At times

more serious issues may arise and this procedure is in place
to provide a mechanism for handling them with love, care
and healing.

8.1   Stages would be:
     a)   involve the members of the pastoral team
     b)   involve two or three deacons (this could follow
         step *c* if agreed by both parties)
     c)   involve a mutually acceptable external person
         or persons
     d)   involve the full deacons board
     e)   involve the church meeting

## 9.   *Period of Appointment*

9.1   This will continue to be on an indefinite basis.
9.2   Guidelines for release to be followed as outlined in
      the church's Principles and Practices.

## 10.   *Development of pastoral team and annual review*

BBC recognises that continuing development of the pastoral
team is vital to the ongoing health and progress of the
kingdom. To assist personal and ministry development, BBC
encourages the pastoral team members to attend courses
and attain qualifications which will assist this process.
Specifically these are the aims of the annual review.

10.1   It should include personal development, training,
      any frustrations, extent of preaching, time outside
      BBC, and how the next year could be improved.
10.2   It should be a stretching and stimulating time which
      contributes greatly to the building up of ministry.
10.3   This is an appraisal process which not only focuses
      on the strengths and abilities of the individual but
      will also focus on those areas which need improve-
      ment and development.

10.4 This review would need to be done within the pastoral team and involve others as agreed by the deacons board.

10.5 It would need to be at a fixed and less busy time in the calendar. The suggested month to begin to process would be January and to be completed by March.

10.6 This review to be initiated by the senior pastor.

10.7 The review of the senior pastor be done by the board chairman and two other deacons chosen by the deacons board.

10.8 The implications of any review would be communicated to those it would seem to be most appropriate.

10.9 More frequent informal reviews will be done particularly with team members in the early years or stages of their ministry.

## 11. Training

11.1 It is expected that one to two weeks of each year would be taken up in training and development activities (e.g. conferences, study, etc.) paid for by the church.

11.2 This should be consistent with the outcome of the annual review and be agreed upon with the senior pastor prior to arrangement.

## 12. Support of Team Members

It is recognised that the pastoral team members are in a particularly vulnerable position and are in need of support preferably from the fellowship. It is our hope that it will be provided in a number of ways:

12.1 The pastoral team should be a place of mutual support for the team members and their spouses.

12.2 It is our hope that each member will have a support

group within twelve months of joining the pastoral team.

12.3 It is suggested that the support group should:

a)  consist of two to four members or friends at BBC (or other people who are in the context of BBC) with the maturity and experience to contribute and support the member.

b)  Meet on a regular basis with the member (e.g. every two or three months).

c)  Give prayerful and practical support, friendship and advice to the member and act as a 'sounding board'.

d)  The prime aims of this group should be personal accountability and encouragement.

12.4 Each member should be involved with a growth group within the pastoral care structure for their personal benefit and for giving an example in the church.

12.5 The deacons board, on behalf of the church, have a vital responsibility for the care of the pastoral team members and their effective working together in ministry. To this end the deacons board will endeavour to care for, encourage, trust and pray for each member of the pastoral team. This will be done through a specific deacon being assigned to the portfolio of each pastoral team member.

12.6 The board chairman, on behalf of the deacons board, is responsible for discussing with the senior pastor how the pastoral team is working, to help to surface any issues.

12.7 The deacon with the equivalent pastoral team ministry portfolio is responsible for contacting and supporting the pastoral team member and to be a resource to them.

13.  *Individuality of team members*

13.1 The above are general guidelines for all pastoral

team members. It is recognised however, that each
member is a unique individual whose needs,
abilities and capacity will differ one from the other.

13.2 Within the general framework of being a good team
member and the responsibility and accountability
which goes along with that, there must also be
allowance for some flexibility.

13.3 The concern of an individual however, must never
become individualistic and so conflict with the
health and unity of the team.

Bramalea Baptist Church: 'where everybody is somebody and Jesus
is Lord'.

# Notes

## Chapter 1

1. Donald Guthrie, *The Pastoral Epistles* (Tyndale, 1973), p. 19.
2. Harold J. Westing, *Multiple Church Staff Handbook* (Kregel, Grand Rapids, 1985), p. 21.

## Chapter 2

1. Mac Anderson, *Successories by Celebrating Excellence* (Successories, Colombus, 1993), pp. 5, 7, 8, 35.
2. A. M. Macdonald, ed., *Chambers Twentieth Century Dictionary* (W. and H. Chambers, 1973), p. 1384.
3. Ben A. Sawatsky, *World Class City Frontier Project Team Training Manual* (Evangelical Free Church Mission, Minneapolis, 1988), p. 6:14.
4. Don Cousins, 'Developing and Managing Leaders and Staff', *The Pastors Update* (Fuller Institute, Pasadena, August, 1990), p. 2662.
5. David Cormack, *Team Spirit: People Working with People* (MARC Europe, 1987), p. 20.
6. Harold J. Westing, *Multiple Church Staff Handbook* (Kregel, Grand Rapids, 1985), pp. 83–5.
7. Ervin F. Henkelmann and Stephen J. Carter, *How to Develop*

NOTES                              189

a *Team Ministry and Make It Work* (Concordia Publishing House, St Louis, 1985), pp. 42–5. Used with permission.
8. Henkelmann and Carter, *How to Develop a Team Ministry*, p. 45.

## Chapter 3

1. Paul Beasley-Murray, *Dynamic Leadership* (MARC Monarch, 1990), p. 185.
2. Eugene B. Habecker, *Rediscovering the Soul of Leadership* (Victor, Wheaton, 1996), p. 11.
3. Calvin Miller, *The Empowered Leader* (Broadman and Holman, Nashville, 1995), p. 7.
4. Paul Hersey and Kenneth H. Blanchard, *Management of Organizational Behavior* (Prentice-Hall, Englewood Cliffs, 1993), p. 5.
5. Warren Bennis and Burt Nanus, *Leaders: The Strategies for Taking Charge* (Harper and Row, New York, 1985), p. 21.
6. Bennis and Nanus, *Leaders*, p. 27.
7. Habecker, *Rediscovering the Soul of Leadership*, p. 12.
8. Paul Hersey, *The Situational Leader* (Center for Leadership Studies, Escondido, 1984), pp. 20–2.
9. Hersey and Blanchard, *M. of O. B.*, pp. 169–201.
   Kenneth Blanchard, Patricia Zigarmi and Drea Zigarmi, *Leadership and the One Minute Manager* (Collins, Glasgow, 1985), p. 30.
10. Hersey and Blanchard, *M. of O. B.*, p. 171.

## Chapter 4

1. T. E. Lawrence, *The Seven Pillars of Wisdom* (Jonathan Cape, 1936), p. 5.
2. Robert Schuller, *Your Church Has Real Possibilities* (Regal, Ventura, 1974), p. 87.
3. James Belasco and Ralph Stayer, *The Flight of the Buffalo* (Warner, New York, 1993), pp. 90–1.

4. Paul Beasley-Murray, *Dynamic Leadership* (MARC Monarch, 1990), p. 184.

5. Warren Bennis and Burt Nanus, *Leaders: The Strategies for Taking Charge* (Harper and Row, New York, 1985), pp. 18, 46, 80.

6. Bennis and Nanus, *Leaders*, pp. 26–79.

7. James Belasco, *Teaching the Elephant to Dance* (Plume, New York, 1990), pp. 2, 4.

8. Lyle E. Schaller, *The Senior Minister* (Abingdon, Nashville, 1989).

9. James Belasco, pp. 17–18.

10. Peter Wagner, *Leading Your Church to Growth* (Regal, Ventura, 1984).

11. Schaller, p. 170.

12. Ray and Anne Ortlund, *Staying Power* (Oliver Nelson, Nashville, 1986), p. 54.

13. Ortlund, *Staying Power*, p. 55.

14. Meyer Friedman and Ray H. Rosenman, *Type A Behavior and Your Heart* (Fawcett Crest, New York, 1974).
See also: Walter McQuade and Ann Aikman, *Stress* (Bantam, New York, 1974), pp. 23–8.

15. Robert R. Blake and Anne Adams McCanse, *Leadership Dilemmas — Grid Solutions* (Gulf Publishing, Houston, 1990), p. 29.

16. Norman Shawchuck, *How To Be a More Effective Church Leader* (Spiritual Growth Resources, Leith, 1990), p. 31.

## Chapter 5

1. Frederick C. Mish, *The New Merriam-Webster Dictionary* (Merriam-Webster, Springfield, 1987), p. 735.

2. Larry Osborne, *The Unity Factor* (Oliver Nelson, Nashville, 1989), p. 17–19.

3. Rick Warren, 'Building a Team Spirit in Your Staff', *The Pastors Update* (Fuller Institute, Pasadena, March 1990), p. 2662.

4. Arthur J. Lange and Patricia Jakubowski, *Responsible Assertive Behavior* (Research Press, Champaign, 1976), p. 7.

5. Peter Drucker, 'Baseball, Business and Teamwork', *Boardroom Reports* (New York, June 1986), p. 9.
6. William G. Kueppers, *Empowering Others and Empowering Yourself* (American Management Association, Watertown, 1991), p. 3.
7. Frank Tillapaugh, *Unleashing the Church* (Regal, Ventura, 1990).
8. Tom Peters, *Thriving on Chaos* (Harper and Row, New York, 1987), p. 510.
9. Rick Warren.

## Chapter 6

1. Don Cousins, 'Developing and Managing Leaders and Staff', *The Pastors Update* (Fuller Institute, Pasadena, August 1990), p. 2662.
2. James M. Shonk, *Working in Teams: A Practical Manual for Improving Work Groups* (American Management Association, New York, 1982), p. 1.
3. John Adair, *Effective Team Building* (Gower Publishing, 1986), p. 39.
4. Myron Rush, *Management: A Biblical Approach* (Victor Books, S. P. Publications, Inc., Wheaton, 1983).
5. Paul Hersey and Kenneth H. Blanchard, *Management of Organizational Behavior* (Prentice-Hall, Englewood Cliffs, 1988).
6. Charles M. Olson, *Cultivating Religious Growth Groups* (Westminster Press, Philadelphia, 1984), pp. 50–3.
7. Mac Anderson, *Successories by Celebrating Excellence* (Successories, Colombus, 1993), p. 32.
8. Anderson, *Successories by Celebrating Excellence*, p. 7.
9. David Cormack, *Team Spirit: People Working with People* (MARC Europe, 1987), p. 106.

## Chapter 7

1. A. M. Macdonald, ed, *Chambers Twentieth Century*

*Dictionary* (W. and H. Chambers, Edinburgh, 1973), pp. 272–3.

2.  Norman Shawchuck, *How to Manage Conflict in the Church: Volume I* (Spiritual Growth Resources, Glendale Heights, 1983), p. 9.
3.  Paul Cedar, 'The Cost of Conflict', *Moody Monthly* (April 1994), p. 12.
4.  Lawrence J. Crabb, *Basic Principles of Biblical Counselling* (Zondervan, Grand Rapids, 1975), pp. 53–80.
    Lawrence J. Crabb, *Institute of Basic Counselling: Training Manual* (Zondervan, Grand Rapids, 1978), pp. 11–13.
5.  Warren Schmidt and Robert Tannenbaum, *The Management of Differences* (McGraw-Hill, New York, 1961), pp. 101–18.
6.  Larry L. McSwain and William C. Treadwell, *Conflict Ministry in the Church* (Broadman, Nashville, 1981), p. 26.
7.  Jerry Robinson and Roy Clifford, *Conflict Management in Community* (University of Illinois, Chicago, 1974).
8.  Norman Shawchuck, *How To Manage Conflict in the Church: Volume 2* (Spiritual Growth Resources, Glendale Heights, 1983), pp. 45–6.
9.  David Cormack, *Peacing Together: From Conflict to Resolution* (MARC Monarch, 1989), p. 56.
10. Cormack, *Peacing Together*, pp. 49–56.

## Chapter 8

1.  David Augsburger, *Caring Enough to Confront* (Herald Press, Scottdale, 1973), pp. 13–17.
2.  Augsburger, *Caring Enough to Confront*, p. 16.
3.  Norman Shawchuck, *How To Manage Conflict in the Church: Volume 1* (Spiritual Growth Resources, Glendale Heights, 1983), pp. 13–19, 21–32.
4.  David W. Johnson and Frank P. Johnson, *Joining Together: Group Therapy and Group Skills* (Prentice-Hall, Englewood Cliffs, 1975), p. 273. Used by permission from David W. Johnson. Reprinted/adapted by permission of Allyn & Bacon.
5.  David Augsburger, *When Caring Is Not Enough: Resolving*

*Conflicts through Fair Fighting* (Regal Books, Ventura, 1983), p. 19. Used by permission.
6. Augsburger, *When Caring Is Not Enough*, p. 19.
7. Augsburger, *When Caring Is Not Enough*, p. 26.
8. Joyce Huggett, *Conflict: Friend or Foe?* (Kingsway, 1984), pp. 43–4.

## Chapter 9

1. David Cormack, *Peacing Together: From Conflict to Resolution* (MARC Monarch, 1989), pp. 35–45.
2. Cormack, *Peacing Together*, p. 45.
3. Cormack, *Peacing Together*, pp. 99–112.
4. Cormack, *Peacing Together*, p. 108.
5. David W. Johnson and Frank P. Johnson, *Joining Together: Group Therapy and Group Skills* (Prentice-Hall, Englewood Cliffs, 1982), p. 285.

## Chapter 10

1. David Cormack, *Peacing Together: From Conflict to Resolution* (MARC Monarch, 1989), p. 152.
2. Norman Shawchuck, *How To Manage Conflict in the Church: Volume 2* (Spiritual Growth Resources, Glendale Heights, 1983), p. 36.
3. A. M. Macdonald, ed., *Chambers Twentieth Century Dictionary* (W. and H. Chambers, 1973), p. 273.
4. Shawchuck.
5. Shawchuck.
6. Shawchuck.

## Leadership Resources

1. © Copyright Ray and Anne Ortlund, *Staying Power* (Oliver Nelson, Nashville, 1986), p. 55. Used by permission.
2. Paul Hersey and Kenneth H. Blanchard, *Management of*

*Organizational Behaviour* (Prentice-Hall, Eaglewood Cliffs, 1993), p. 182. Adapted with permission from the Center for Leadership Studies. Situation Leadership ® is a registered trademark of Center for Leadership Studies, Escondido, California. All rights reserved.